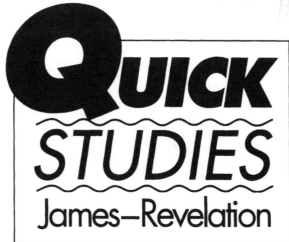

Cook Ministry Resources
a division of Cook Communications Ministries
Colorado Springs, Colorado/Paris, Ontario

800-708-5550
800-923-7543

The following authors and editors contributed to his volume:

Stan Campbell
John Duckworth
Jim Townsend, Ph.D.

Quick Studies
James through Revelation

Unless otherwise noted, Scripture quotations are from the Holy Bible, New International Version (NIV), © 1973, 1978, 1984 by International Bible Society. Used by permission of Zondervan Bible Publishers.

Cook Ministry Resources
a division of Cook Communications Ministries
4050 Lee Vance View
Colorado Springs, CO 80918-7100
Cable address: DCCOOK
Designed by Bill Paetzold
Cover illustrations by Steve Björkman
Inside illustrations by Michael Fleishman and Jack DesRocher
Printed in U.S.A.

ISBN: 0-7814-0029-5

JUDE

REVELATION

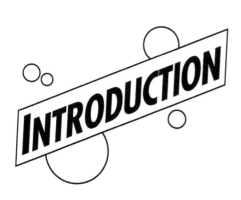

Quick Questions about Quick Studies

We've made *Quick Studies* as self-explanatory as possible, so you can dive in and start using them right away. But just in case you were wondering . . .

When should I use *Quick Studies*?

Whenever you want high school or junior high kids to explore the Bible face-to-face and absorb it into their lives. We've kept the openers active and the discussion questions creative, so you can use *Quick Studies* with confidence in Sunday school, midweek youth Bible study, small groups, even youth group meetings and retreats.

What's so quick about *Quick Studies*?

They're designed to save you preparation time. The session plans are compact, for quick reading. There aren't a lot of materials to gather, either (you'll need Bibles, pencils and paper, copies of the reproducible sheets, and sometimes a few other items). Yet *Quick Studies* are *real* Bible studies, with plenty of thought-provoking discussion and life application.

How are these different from other youth Bible studies?

We like to think *Quick Studies* are . . .

• *Irresistible.* You already know most kids don't jump at the chance to fill in a bunch of blanks in a boring study guide. So we used creative, reproducible sheets and *active* activities to draw kids into Scripture.

• *Involving.* You need discussion *starters*, not discussion *stoppers*. We avoided dull "yes or no" questions and included lots of thought-provokers that should get your group members talking about important issues. And we didn't forget suggested *answers* to most of the tougher questions, which should make things easier for you.

• *Inductive.* Many Bible studies try to force-feed kids a single "aim" and ignore other points Scripture is trying to make. *Quick Studies* let kids discover a variety of key principles in a passage.

• *Influential.* It's not enough to know what the Bible says. Every session includes a step designed to help kids decide what to do *personally* with vital points from the chapter.

When do kids read the passages covered?

That's up to you. If your group is into homework, assign the passages in advance. If not, take time to read the Scripture together after the "Opening Act" step that kicks off each session. There are dozens of ways to read a passage—with volunteers taking turns, or with a narrator and actors "performing" a scene, or with kids underlining points as they read silently, or with you reading as the author and kids listening as the original audience, or with small groups paraphrasing as they read . . .

What if I want to cover more—or less—than a chapter in a session?

Quick Studies is flexible. Each 45- to 60-minute session covers a chapter of the New Testament, but you can adjust the speed to fit your group. To cover more than one chapter in a session, just pick the points you want to emphasize and drop the activities, questions, and reproducible sheets you don't need. To cover less than a chapter, you may need to add a few questions and spend more time discussing the "So What?" application step in detail.

Do I have to cover a whole New Testament book?

No. Each session stands alone. Use sessions one at a time if you want to, or mix and match books in any order you choose. No matter how you use them, *Quick Studies* are likely to help your group see Bible study in a whole new light.

John Duckworth, Series Editor

JAMES 1

Passing Your Tests

As God provides wisdom, we begin to see that even our trials and testing of faith are opportunities to develop spiritual maturity. God isn't behind the temptations we face, so we should stand strong against them. In fact, God is the source of everything good. Therefore, we should not just know what He wants us to do, but we should also act on what we know.

(Needed: Whistle, bell, or some other kind of signal)

Form teams. Have a relay race in which individuals must walk from one end of the room to the other and back. The catch is that each time you blow a whistle (or give some other signal), each walker must stop and turn 90 degrees to the left or right, then wait for the next signal before walking in the new direction. See how long it takes the first two walkers to make it back to their teams. Chances are that it will take so long that you'll want to call off the race after the first two or four walkers. Then discuss how hard it is to make progress when you keep changing your mind—an idea addressed in the first chapter of James.

DATE I USED THIS SESSION _____ GROUP I USED IT WITH _____

NOTES FOR NEXT TIME _____

_____

_____

WHAT DOES JAMES SAY ABOUT TRIALS? (v 1-4)
- Attitude of JOY
- Xtns go thru trials "brethren"
- It's goig to happen
- Various
- reason - i.e. tests our faith

④a ④b WHAT DO YOU DO WHEN Don't know WHO Do YOU TURN TO IF Don't KNOW WHAT TO DO?

WHAT DOES THE BIBLE SAY (v 5-8)

① Money Amounts Assigned to ea. kid
② Arrange ea. other according to **value** - least to most importance
③ Why - What does our culture SAY is valuable? important?
④ What does the bible SAY
⑤ Places - ⑥ WHAT IS THE CAUSE OF TEMPTATION?

Ⓧ Drama- hand in Ants nest, Choking me out
- punch in nose
- hide in car on date
- took rings

1. **What's the worst thing that's happened to you recently? In spite of it, did *anything* positive result as well?** (Failing a test might improve study habits in the long run; the death of a relative might bring the family closer; breaking up with someone might create better dating opportunities, etc. If nothing else, each negative experience we get through makes us a little stronger to handle the next one.) **Do verses 2-4 make more sense in light of this? Why or why not?**

2. **If you lacked wisdom** (vs. 5), **how would you know it?** (Unable to make a decision; things seem to be falling apart around you, etc.) **Can you think of any time when you *don't* lack wisdom? What's the first thing you do when you face a problem and don't know what to do?** (Most of us usually try to handle our problems ourselves, not realizing that God "gives generously to all without finding fault.")

3. **Let's say you have three choices of what to do after you graduate: college, community college, or the military. You make a list of pros and cons for each choice, but come up with the same number for all three. What should you do** (vss. 6-8)**?** (Pray for wisdom and believe that God has given it to you. After listening to the advice of others, make up your mind and stick with it until you've given that option a chance.)

4. **Do you think it would be a "trial" to have lots of money? Explain.** (See verses 9-11. If our goal is to have God provide for our needs, money could get in the way. That's why those "in humble circumstances" can "take pride." Yet rich people with the proper attitude also please God. So we decide if money [a little or a lot] brings us closer to God, or becomes an obstacle in our relationships with Him.)

5. **Why does God tempt us?** (This is a trick question. God never tempts us [vss. 13-15]. He's the source of *good* things [vss. 16-18]. Yet He allows us to be tempted because resisting temptation makes us stronger Christians.)

6. **Look at verses 19-21. What percentage of your conflicts might be avoided if you or the other person weren't so quick to "fly off the handle"?** (Discuss the need to be slow to speak and slow to become angry.)

7. One morning you wake up and go to the mirror. You see hair that looks like birds are nesting there, drool coming from the corners of your mouth, and a nose that needs blowing. What would other people think if you ignored everything you saw and went to school just the way you were? What do you think God and fellow Christians think when you look in the Bible and see changes you need to make, but don't make them? (Discuss the mirror principle in verses 22-25.)

8. Look at verses 26 and 27. Which of the following would be hardest for you: (a) giving up swearing for a week; (b) saying only encouraging things for a week; (c) giving a week's pay or allowance to a fund for widows and orphans; or (d) giving up TV and movies for a week? Why? What might you get out of trying each of these?

Have small groups work on the reproducible sheet, "Rap Gaps," as a review. Some blanks are tougher than others to fill in; there are no "right" answers. Then have each group write an additional stanza on the back of the sheet, showing a specific way to live out one of James' pieces of advice. Finally, have groups perform their raps for each other.

Yo! Listen, everybody, and you'll find out
What James chapter 1 is all about.
If you're facing trials, whether girl or boy,
Consider all your testing a very _____.

When you face a decision and don't know what's best,
Just look up to heaven and _____, and that's what
For _____ gives _____ or you won't be freed.
you need,
But do not _____.

If you find yourself in a humble place,
You can put a _____ upon your face
'Cause riches soon will pass away,
And _____.

Are you being tempted? Then do not say, _____!"
"For God tempts no one, His gifts are good,
So _____.

Remember this in the coming week:
Be quick to listen and _____
It does no good to _____
Accept the Word and _____

When it comes to the Word, are you just a hearer?
That's like _____
And then he leaves with his face still messed;
Do what you hear and _____

If you think you're a pretty outstanding believer
But your tongue's on the loose, you're _____, too,
_____
Take care of _____
And don't let the world _____

This James guy packed an awful lot into his first chapter. To help you keep all his advice straight, try coming up with a rap. We've done parts of it for you; see whether you can fill in the gaps.

JAMES 2

No Seating Chart

Churches should be free from discrimination and favoritism, especially in regard to wealth. We need to go beyond mere words in expressing our faith. Real faith in God is confirmed with loving actions toward each other. So-called faith without actions is "dead."

Have kids take the "Are You Good Enough for This Group?" test on the reproducible sheet. Then seat kids according to their scores—highest scores in front, lowest in back. Explain that it's pretty easy to tell when we're being discriminated against. James challenges us to make sure we aren't guilty of showing favoritism—especially at church.

DATE I USED THIS SESSION _____ GROUP I USED IT WITH _____

NOTES FOR NEXT TIME _____

_____

_____

1. Have you ever gone somewhere and realized that just about everyone else was dressed more nicely than you were? How were you treated?

2. What kinds of shoes, jackets, and hairstyles could cause you to be discriminated against if you wore them to school? To church? What kinds might cause people to treat you better at school? At church?

3. Be honest: Do you think you ever show favoritism? In what ways? How would you explain this to James?

4. We all should avoid treating one group of people better or worse than another, but it's especially important for the church not to play favorites. **Why** (vss. 1-7)? (God is willing to accept anyone into His kingdom. When we show more respect for one group than another, we portray God as judgmental and unfair.)

5. Is it possible to "Love your neighbor as yourself" (vs. 8) **without doing anything to show it? How have you shown it?**

6. Look at verses 10-13. Do you ever find yourself thinking, "Sure, I'm not perfect, but at least I don't . . ."? If you divided the Ten Commandments (Exodus 20) **into what most people would call "OK sins" and "serious sins," how would your list look?** (Emphasize that sin is sin. James's point was that people excused their tendency to play favorites, thinking, "Well, at least it's not murder or adultery.")

7. When we see others in need, we might choose to help. Or we might choose to ignore them. But there's another option as well. **What is it** (vss. 14-17)? (We can say we want to help, yet not actually do anything.)

8. Why is it such a problem when Christians decide on the third option? (We talk a lot about faith, but if people see that all we do is talk, we don't represent God very well. Our faith in Him should result in action.)

9. Do you think James was saying that faith wasn't important—that as long as we do good things for others that God will save us (vss. 18, 19)? **Explain.** (His emphasis on deeds was *in response to* salvation by grace through faith. He points out one level of "faith" that God exists, which even the demons have. But genuine, saving faith should motivate believers to action.)

10. James reminds us that both Abraham (vss. 20-24) and Rahab (vss. 25, 26) showed faith in God which was reflected in their actions. If people never heard a word you said about God or what you believed, and only saw your actions, do you think they would detect God at work in your life? **Explain.** (Summarize the importance of faith and actions working together [vs. 22].)

11. If actions speak louder than words, is your life a whisper, a mumble, a shout, or a rock concert? How can you "crank up the volume"?

James gives us a picture of a "faithful" Christian walking up to another believer who happens to be poor and hungry and saying, "Go, I wish you well; keep warm and well fed" (2:16). But then the Christian walks away without helping in any way. Pretty ridiculous, huh? What *should* the Christian have done? Let's see how many ideas we can come up with—but they have to be actions, not words. In fact, let's make them things you could do for a needy person without saying a single word. Brainstorm as many ideas as you can. Then, if possible, plan as a group to carry out at least one of them.

ARE YOU GOOD ENOUGH FOR THIS GROUP?

We have to be very careful about whom we let into this group, you know. Please fill out this form to help us decide whether you're good enough for us.

1. Are you related to anyone important?
   ❏ The President of the United States (10 points)
   ❏ Anybody on MTV (5 points)
   ❏ The guy who cleans up after "The Singing Dogs" (1 point)

2. How much money are you willing to give our group each week?
   ❏ $1,000 or more (10 points)
   ❏ $500 or more (5 points)
   ❏ All the pennies I happen to have in my pocket (1 point)

3. How "cool" are you?
   ❏ So cool that my agent wants me to do some "Gap" ads (10 points)
   ❏ So cool that companies name cars after me (5 points)
   ❏ So cool that I know the words to the *Brady Bunch* theme (1 point)

4. Do you have any flaws?
   ❏ Just a beauty mark on my finely chiseled chin (10 points)
   ❏ One eyebrow is slightly more perfect than the other (5 points)
   ❏ No, my 24 toes are all quite attractive (1 point)

5. What kind of jewelry are you wearing?
   ❏ Only gold, platinum, and diamonds (10 points)
   ❏ Only gold, platinum, and cubic zirconium (5 points)
   ❏ Only a plastic ring from a Wal-Mart vending machine (1 point)

6. How smart are you?
   ❏ Smart enough to ace the SAT in my sleep (10 points)
   ❏ Smart enough to get into Clown College (5 points)
   ❏ Could you repeat the question? (1 point)

7. What awards have you won?
   ❏ A Nobel Prize, Pulitzer Prize, or Academy Award (10 points)
   ❏ Miss Teenage America or Mr. Universe (5 points)
   ❏ A gold star for eating all my spinach (1 point)

8. What celebrity do you look most like?
   ❏ Any rock star except Axl Rose (10 points)
   ❏ Any movie star except Benji (5 points)
   ❏ Huckleberry Hound (1 point)

If your answer is "Other" for any of these questions, give yourself no points for that question.

TOTAL POINTS _____

JAMES 3

Licking a Problem

There are a lot of ways to sin, but one of the most common sources of trouble is the "tongue." Controlling the things we say is just about the hardest challenge we have as Christians. We also need to ensure that the wisdom we desire is based on humility rather than jealousy or selfish desires.

Cut the four skit scenarios from the reproducible sheet, "Conversation Starters." Give each to a pair of kids. These pairs must improvise conversations based on their characters and settings, using the first and last lines listed. Each conversation must last for at least 30 seconds, and no longer than a minute. Note that two of the skits start negatively and end the same way; the other two move from negative to positive. After kids perform the skits, discuss: **Why is it hard to stop a war of words, to turn a negative conversation into a positive one? Why is it easy to let a conversation stay negative?** Point out that this chapter is largely concerned with the negative and positive things we say.

DATE I USED THIS SESSION _____ GROUP I USED IT WITH _____

NOTES FOR NEXT TIME _____

_____

_____

1. Think of the teachers you've disliked. What do they have in common? How about the teachers you've liked?

2. What's the worst that can happen if a teacher doesn't do a good job? (The teacher could get fired; worse, a young person could fall behind the rest of the class or think that learning and education are boring and unimportant.) Why is teaching even more important in church than elsewhere (vss. 1, 2)? (Pastors, Sunday school teachers, and others speak for God concerning issues of eternal importance. God will hold them accountable for what they say.)

3. What influences you more: the things you *hear* a youth leader tell you, or the things you can *see* for yourself in his or her life? Give an example. Which do you think is the easier method of teaching? (It's not so hard to *say* the right things; "practicing what we preach" is usually much more difficult.)

4. Look at verse 2. How many sins can you think of that involve the words we use? (Lying, boasting, hypocrisy, flattery, slander, gossip, profanity, etc.) Have you ever said something you wished you hadn't? Which of those sins did it involve?

5. James uses several visual images to describe the power our tongues have (vss. 3-8). How could your words be powerful enough to . . .

* Steer a friend into trouble as a bit steers a horse?
* Influence the direction of this meeting as a rudder guides a ship?
* Ruin a teacher's reputation as a fire does a forest?
* Poison a relationship with a parent?

6. What percentage of your words are probably positive? Negative? Why is a mixture a problem (vss. 9-12)? (Our words are sometimes uplifting, sometimes destructive. Those who listen to us are like people going to a spring and getting fresh water one time, salt water the next. We need to be consistently "pure" with our words.)

7. Why do you think people aren't able (or willing) to control the things they say to each other? Do you think it's easier for Christians to control their speech than for nonbelievers? Explain.

8. Some people say the "smart" thing to do is to use words to get ahead in the world. Say what people want to hear, and position yourself to move up. Do you think that works? What's the problem with this kind of "wisdom" (vss. 13-18)? (It is "earthly, unspiritual, [and] of the devil.")

9. If you had to hire two famous actors, one to dramatically read verses 14-16 and one to read verses 17 and 18, who would they be? Why?

10. Which signs of heavenly wisdom (humility, purity, peacemaking, consideration, submission, mercy, impartiality, sincerity, etc.) do you see least at school? Which do you see most? Explain.

Consider letting teams of students rotate as "Speech Police" for the next month or so. Make them responsible for noting positive and negative speech of the other group members, perhaps bestowing them with power to give "citations" for offenses and rewards for positive examples. If your young people aren't watching what they're saying when in your meetings, they certainly aren't doing it elsewhere. Try to get the positive patterns started here, and maybe they will spread to home, school, work, and elsewhere.

CONVERSATION
STARTERS

SKIT 1: Clash Reunion

Characters: Two young men or women.
Place: At a class reunion.
First line: "Hey, I haven't seen you since you stole my girlfriend [or boyfriend] when we were in school."
Last line: "See you in another 10 years—but not if I can help it."

SKIT 2: Team Rivalry

Characters: Two softball players on opposing teams.
Place: On the field, just before a game.
First line: "I hear your team is the worst in the league."
Last line: "Let's get together after the game for some pizza."

SKIT 3: Fashion Fight

Characters: Two freshmen in high school.
Place: First class of the day.
First line: "Where did you find that outfit—at the circus?"
Last line: "Now look what you did. We're both going to the principal's office."

SKIT 4: Ticket Taker

Characters: Two friends.
Place: In the car on the way to a concert.
First line: "How could you lose the concert tickets? I can't believe anybody could be so dumb."
Last line: "I take back what I said. Let's just go rent a video, OK?"

JAMES 4

A Cracked Crystal Ball

Our selfish desires create many problems for us—fights, arguments, bad habits, disappointments, and more. The solution to these problems is to learn to submit to God rather than stubbornly demanding our own way. We should treat each other with respect, and not take the future for granted—since we have no guarantee of being here tomorrow.

(Needed: Kitchen timer, bag, board game or other game)

Form teams to play a game like volleyball, basketball, or a board game. Before you start, though, ask for a volunteer. This person will stick his or her hand in a bag, where you've put a kitchen timer, and turn the dial on the timer—thereby determining how long the game will last. Nobody will know how long the game will be, but whoever's ahead when the timer goes off will be the winner. Use this later as an illustration of the fact that none of us knows when his or her life will end, despite our plans and boasting (vss. 13-17).

DATE I USED THIS SESSION _____ GROUP I USED IT WITH _____

NOTES FOR NEXT TIME _____

_____

_____

1. Who do you seem to fight with most often? What's most likely to "set you off"? How many times out of ten would you say the conflict is your fault? The other person's fault? Nobody's fault?

2. When people want something but can't seem to get it by asking nicely, what other methods do they use to get it? (Demanding; manipulating; shoplifting or otherwise stealing; cheating; going to war, etc.) What "wants" do you think led to (a) the American Civil War; (b) the Vietnam War; (c) the Persian Gulf War?

3. James says selfish desires are the source of our fights (vss. 1, 2), and that we should ask God for what we want. What if you've tried asking God for what you want, but you didn't get it? What might be your problem? (God promises to provide for our every need, not our every want. If we ask with selfish motives, we shouldn't expect a positive answer to every request. Other times requests may not be selfish, but God knows why granting them would not be best for us and for His kingdom.)

4. After accusing his readers of being quarrelsome, James calls them "adulterous" (vs. 4.) How do you feel about all these charges? Are they fair? (We're all selfish enough to start fights. As for "adulterous," James probably means that his readers [and we] tend to be spiritually unfaithful, loving the world more than we love God [vss. 4-6].)

5. Sometimes even Christians are lured into loving sin rather than loving God. What if you realize that you're fighting for the wrong side, and you want to come back to God (vss. 7-10)? (The more we "come near" to God, the easier it is to resist the devil. We need to purify our hands [actions] and hearts [attitudes], asking His forgiveness. It's tough to forsake the "fun" our friends may live for, and live for God instead, but it's worth the reward.)

6. A friend sees verse 9 and says, "Yep, just like I thought. Christians never get to have a good time—or even laugh at a joke." What do you say? (This kind of mourning is part of repenting—turning from sin and being sorry for your offense against God. Then comes the real joy and laughing, after the Lord lifts you up [vs. 10].)

7. **What are some ways that we in this group might "speak against" each other** (vss. 11-12)**?** (Through gossip, jealous comments, judgmental statements, etc.) **Why is this a big deal?** (Judging hurts your relationship with others and with God as well.)

8. **Do you think Christians should talk to God about everything they plan to do?** (God probably has given most of us the ability to choose what to eat for breakfast, for instance, without asking His advice. But He knows the future and we don't. Any guidance we can get from Him will help us make better decisions about what we want to do.)

9. **What's the right way to make plans** (vss. 13-17)**?** (Instead of saying, "I'm going to be a doctor," "I'm going to spend a year in France," or whatever, we need to think in terms of what we'll do "if it is the Lord's will.")

10. **What does verse 17 have to do with verses 13-16?** (Since we don't know how long we have to live, we shouldn't put off doing what we know we should do.) **What's the most important thing you can do for your best friend this week? For your parents? For your youth leader?**

Have kids think about their attitudes toward planning, using the reproducible sheet, "Back-up Plans." When they finish, discuss: **How do you feel about the fact that you can't completely plan your life? How do feel about the idea that God knows and wants what's best for you? If someday you realize that He may be leading you away from a plan you've had for a long time, do you think you'd be willing to change course?**

BACK-UP
PLANS

Some kids can tell you the college they plan to attend, what their major will be, the date of graduation, the kind of person they'll marry, the color of the house they'll buy, and how many children they expect to have. Others can't tell you what they plan to do between now and dinner, much less with the rest of their lives.

Which group are you in? Circle each category in which you have any plans at all.

What I'm going to have for lunch tomorrow

What I'll wear to church next week

Whether I'll get married

The next thing I'll buy

My next *major* purchase

When I'll take my driver's test (or get my next car)

Whether I'll make a speech at graduation

Whether I'll go to college

Where I'll go to college

Where I'll live when I retire

What my first job will be

What my job will be in 10 years

The next thing I'll say

Whether I'll ever have my name in the paper

What classes I'll take next semester

What I'll watch on TV tonight

The next argument I'll have

The next song I'll sing

What I'll do right after this meeting

How much money I'll have in six months

Where my first bank account will be

The next present I'll give someone

Whether I'll be on any teams next year

Whether I'll be on the honor roll next year

How I'll get my next date

Whether my hair will ever be gray

How tall I'll be in five years

Whether I'll travel to a foreign country by the time I'm out of school

Whether I'll get something in my eye in the next five minutes

Now for the important part. You don't know whether you'll be around to do these things. Only God does. That's why it's so important, when you plan, to say to yourself, "These are things I'd like to do *if it is the Lord's will*" (James 4:15). Go back through the list and put a check mark (√) beside each item where you've done this.

JAMES 5

Wealthy? Who, Me?

Rich people who mistreat others will eventually pay for their proud, sinful attitudes. What we currently consider as "wealth" will not have lasting value in eternity. So rather than regret what we don't have, believers need to be patient with each other as we live for God. We should speak clearly and follow through on what we say. We should also be prayerful and help each other remain faithful whenever we can.

Hand out copies of the reproducible sheet, "Copier Clowns." Let kids spend a couple of minutes trying to find the "two alike" clowns. Then let them in on the secret—all the clowns are exactly alike. Talk about the frustration of trying to solve this puzzle, and the letdown of knowing that you can't trust the directions. Mention that you'll discuss two "frustrations" in this chapter—the need for patience, and the difficulty of unanswered prayer. When we're frustrated with the Bible's instructions, we may think they're wrong, too.

DATE I USED THIS SESSION _____ GROUP I USED IT WITH _____

NOTES FOR NEXT TIME _____

_____

_____

1. Do you think rich people are happy? What makes you think so?

2. If you had a source of money that never ran out, do you think you'd ever be satisfied with what you had? **Explain.** (There's always something else to buy. If money were no object, some people would never set limits—and would probably never be satisfied.)

3. We all know the "plus" sides of being rich—or think we do. But what's the down side of having lots of money (vss. 1-5)? (As the cost of a wealthy lifestyle continues to rise, many people become a lot more protective of what they own. They depend on having lots of money come in on a regular basis. They may underpay the people who work for them and apply most of their income to their own selfish desires.)

4. How would you (or would you) match the following situations to phrases in verses 2-6: (a) A rich man loses most of his money in a stock market crash; (b) a factory leaves toxic waste in the ground, and it leaks into the local water supply; (c) workers die in a fire because a building owner didn't install a sprinkler system; (d) a "sweat shop" hires illegal aliens who can't complain even though they are paid half the minimum wage?

5. Christians are called to be patient. What does patience have to do with our financial condition (vss. 7-11)? (If we're living for God, we won't see all our rewards until after our earthly lives are over. It takes patience to see so many people wasting money if we have little. But Jesus will return, and we need to live as if it will be today.)

6. Verse 12 is about saying things like "I swear it," not about using profanity. What does this have to do with you? (We need to live so that when we say yes to something, people know we'll do it. When we say no, we should mean no.)

7. When was the last time you were "in trouble" (vs. 13)? Did you pray? Other than saying, "Help!" what could you have prayed?

8. When was the last time you sang a praise song *outside* of church (vs. 13)? What would be the best place for you to do this?

9. Have you ever prayed that someone would get well, and he or she didn't? How did you feel? How can verses 14-16 be true, when prayers for the sick don't always "work"? (There are at least three explanations offered for this. Some say it should work, and when it doesn't someone involved lacks faith. Others say that it isn't always God's will to heal [see Paul's experience in II Corinthians 12:7-10], and that we should pray, "If it be Your will." Still others say that the Greek words translated "sick" and "sick person" actually refer to spiritual weakness, not physical illness.)

10. Do you know the other people in this group well enough to confess sins to them (vs. 16)? Do you know them well enough to know whether they're wandering from the truth (vss. 19, 20)? Explain. How could we make this the kind of group where these verses can be acted out?

You may not have all the money in the world. You may not have all the money you want. You may not even have bus fare to get across town. But you've got something better. You have the privilege of prayer, which will let God know exactly what you need. Let's brainstorm a list of the things you need. Using the categories from James 5:13-16, make three columns for your list: Trouble in My Life; Things I'm Happy About; People Who Need Healing. Then spend some time praying about these requests and praises.

COPIER CLOWNS

These clowns may all look similar, but only two of them are exactly alike. Can you spot them?

I PETER 1

Strangers in Danger

Peter writes to "scattered" Christians in various provinces with a message of praise and hope. He reminds his readers that what God has given us can never be destroyed. So when we face suffering, we should never forget that it's only temporary. Therefore, we should be holy, live for God, and love one another from the heart.

(Needed: Team prize [optional])

Form teams of at least three kids. At your signal, each team is to discover something that makes one of its members different from the rest—and set that person apart by sending him or her to a designated spot in the room. For example, two of the kids might like pickles, but the third one hates pickles. Two might have traveled out-of-state, but the third hasn't. The team to "set apart" the "different" person first is the winner of that round. Play several rounds. Award a team prize if you like. (If you have fewer than six kids, form just one team and award a prize to the "most different" kid.) Then talk about how it felt to be different, to be set apart. This chapter has a lot to say about that subject.

DATE I USED THIS SESSION _____ GROUP I USED IT WITH _____

NOTES FOR NEXT TIME _____

_____

_____

1. When have you felt the most out of place? Does it bother you to be different from people around you, or are you the "I've got to be me" type? Explain.

2. I Peter was written when Christians were "strangers in the world" for the first time. People would come to Jerusalem on business, hear about and believe in Jesus, then go back home (vss. 1, 2). **What problems might you expect these "strangers" to face? How is this like being in a youth group for a couple of hours a week, and being at school for five days a week?** (We're "strangers in the world" most of the time, too.)

3. If you go off to camp for a couple of weeks and start to get homesick, the counselor will probably tell you that (1) your home is still there and everything is OK, and (2) your stay at camp is only temporary, and you'll be home soon. **How is that like verses 3-7?** (Note the positive words Peter uses: *great mercy*, *new birth*, *living hope*, *resurrection*, *inheritance*, *shielded*, *salvation*, etc. Even our sufferings, he says, intensify our faith in God.)

4. Since you can't see God (vss. 8, 9)**, how do you keep in mind that He exists and loves you?** (Examples: Prayer; Bible study; sensitivity to the Holy Spirit; fellowship, in order to see Him at work in the lives of others.)

5. What advantage do you have over the Old Testament prophets (vss. 10-12)**?** (They brought the message that God would send a Messiah, but couldn't fully understand what was going to happen.) **What advantage do you have over angels?** (They can't really know what it's like to be saved from sin through the death of Jesus [vs. 12].) **What should our response be to all these advantages (vss. 13-16)?** (We're to "be holy"—to set ourselves apart from evil in the world, but not from its people.)

6. On a scale of 1 (least) to 10 (most), how would you rate yourself on: being prepared to do right; self-control; hope; obedience; holiness?

7. Suppose you went to spend a year in another country as part of a student exchange program. Do you think you'd act better or worse around your hosts than you do around your parents? Explain. (Discuss the concept of living as "strangers" in the world until we get "home" with God [vs. 17].)

8. What does it mean to live "in reverent fear" before God (vs. 17)? How can you love someone you're scared of? (If we experience God's perfect love, we shouldn't be afraid to approach Him or ask for things [I John 4:18]. The kind of "fear" we need is really respect. We should maintain reverence and respect for God at all times. [See vss. 18-21.])

9. What are three things you've done this week to show or tell other people that you love them (vs. 22)?

10. How do you feel when you read verses 24 and 25? How long would you live on earth if it were up to you? Since it isn't, how can you best prepare for the next life?

Have kids take the quiz on the reproducible sheet, "Out of Place." (Answers: 1[d], since the rest are dances; 2[c], since the rest have to do with Halloween; 3[c], as the rest are cars [including the antique Stanley Steamer]; 4[a], as the rest are mentioned in I Peter 1:1; 5[d], since the rest are to be a normal part of the Christian life; 6[c], as the rest are "perishable"; 7[a], 8[b], 9[c], 10[d], as we are to be set apart from evil desires [vs. 14].) After discussing the quiz, ask: **What's the hardest "crowd activity" for you to give up? Why? Do you think God expects too much of us? Do you think we are expected to be holy mainly to make God look good to others, or more for our own good? Why?**

OUT of PLACE

Which item in each list doesn't belong with the rest?

1.
a. Salsa
b. Lambada
c. Watusi
d. Pygmy

2.
a. Pumpkin
b. Bat
c. Turkey
d. Mask

3.
a. Pinto
b. Mustang
c. Lodestone
d. Steamer

4.
a. Ephesus
b. Pontus
c. Galatia
d. Cappadocia

5.
a. Holiness
b. Happiness
c. Suffering
d. Ignorance

6.
a. Silver
b. Gold
c. Word of God
d. Ham sandwich

7.
a. You
b. Gossip
c. Putdowns
d. Racial jokes

8.
a. Drugs
b. You
c. Alcohol
d. Speeding

9.
a. Revenge
b. Violence
c. You
d. Grudges

10.
a. Pornographic magazines
b. "Adult" video
c. "900 number" phone "sex" lines
d. You

I PETER 2

Rocks That Roll

Only by remembering what we mean to God can we prepare ourselves to face rejection by the rest of the world. We are a chosen people, a royal priesthood, a holy nation, a people belonging to God, and "living stones" that are being built into a spiritual house. With this in mind, we should submit ourselves to earthly authorities—even those who cause us to suffer unjustly. Like Jesus, we should not retaliate, and instead leave the judging to God.

(Needed: Team prizes [optional])

Have teams compete to do their "impressions" of famous structures: the Sears Tower, the Leaning Tower of Pisa, the Statue of Liberty, the Superdome, the pyramids of Egypt, etc. Each team will need a "building foreman" to arrange team members in the desired shape. Award prizes for the best impressions if you like. Later, explain that God is shaping us into a building as well, though His work is sure to be sturdier than our own.

DATE I USED THIS SESSION _____ GROUP I USED IT WITH _____

NOTES FOR NEXT TIME _____

_____

_____

Q&A

1. If someone forced you to run a race where you were the only one wearing wrist and ankle weights, how would you react? As we run the Christian "race," what are some of the ways in which we weigh *ourselves* down? (Compare answers with the list in verse 1.)

2. Peter had recently reminded his readers that they had been "born again" (1:23). **As a result, what is one of the things they need right away** (2:2, 3)**? Why?** (They [and we] should instinctively crave "pure spiritual milk" to fulfill the desire to grow spiritually.) **Do you crave anything more than you want God's Word? Why do you think that is?** (Maybe we haven't really "tasted that the Lord is good" [vs. 3] and need to give Him a try.)

3. We should grow not only as individuals, but as a group. We're described as living stones who all fit together to form a house that God lives in (vss. 4, 5). Jesus is the cornerstone of the house (vs. 6). **Is our "group house" more like a cathedral, a mud hut, a shack, or the place you live in? Why?**

4. When people reject Christ, He's like a stone over which they stumble (vss. 7, 8). **In what ways do people get tripped up when they don't depend on Jesus to set their lives straight?** (They can't find peace with God; they try to work their way to God but can't obey the law completely; they stay lost in their sins. The only answer, Jesus, remains right in front of them—but they keep stumbling.)

5. In addition to being "living stones," we are "a royal priesthood" (vss. 5, 9). **What were the duties of a priest that might apply to us?** (Be a model of holiness; offer sacrifices; intercede for others, etc.)

6. Since we are "a people belonging to God" (vss. 9, 10), **how should we interact with "worldly" people who don't belong to God** (vss. 11, 12)**?** (It might seem that we should avoid them, but it becomes more important than ever to set good examples around them so they can see God at work in our lives.)

7. God wants us to faithfully serve those in authority over us (vss. 13-17). **Which of the following make you want to *not* obey authorities: (a) schoolwide locker searches for drugs; (b) dress codes; (c) being bored in class; or (d) not respecting individual teachers or principals? Explain.**

8. If you're a Christian, **what should you do if you have a teacher, boss, parent, or some other authority who is downright unfair** (vss. 18-20)? (That's when we should be most submissive [as long as the problem is unfairness, not abuse or telling us to do something wrong]. If we serve God, we can't count on things being "fair." We're challenged to "bear up" when faced with unjust suffering.)

9. When you recall what Jesus suffered for you (vss. 21-25)**, does it make it harder or easier to tell Him about the things you have to suffer? Why?** (Jesus' suffering was much harder than what most of us go through, but He still wants us to talk to Him about our problems and needs. He knows exactly how we feel *because* He suffered so much.)

One way to endure unjust suffering is to realize that we're not alone in our feelings. The reproducible sheet, "Bear Up," asks kids to show how they feel about the authority figures in their lives. Without allowing the use of names or specifics, have everyone share as much as possible. As they do, make a list of unfair situations mentioned. Then go through the list and ask: **What do you think Jesus would have done if He were in this situation?**

Bear Up

What authorities are toughest for you to "bear"? After each of the following people who exercise some kind of power over you, circle the grizzly bear (tough) or the teddy bear (easy) to show how hard it usually is for you to accept that person's authority. If some of the people don't apply to you, write in some who do.

1. Mall security guards

2. Your youth leader

3. The President of the United States

4. Your principal

5. Your P.E. teacher or coach

6. Police officers

7. Your band leader, choir director, or music teacher

8. Your father

9. Your mother

10. The chairman of the Federal Communications Commission

11. Your congressional representatives

12. Your English teacher

13. Your pastor

14. Your boss

15. Your doctor

16. Your dentist

17. Your science teacher

18. Your math teacher

19. Your stepfather

20. Your stepmother

I PETER 3

The Beautiful People

Peter's previous challenge to be submissive as Christians to our leaders and bosses (chapter 2) is here applied to husbands and wives. The true beauty of a woman, he says, is a gentle, quiet, godly spirit. Husbands are to be considerate of wives as well. All Christians should be eager to do good and ready to give the reason for the hope we have.

(Needed: Sheet, blanket, or cardboard with three holes in it)

Conduct a beauty contest. But rather than judging the entire person, select one trait at a time. Have three volunteers compete at a time, sticking only their right ears, left feet, knees, or elbows through holes in a sheet or other screen that you hold up. Let the rest of the group be the judges. After a few rounds, begin the session by discussing what true beauty is.

DATE I USED THIS SESSION _____ GROUP I USED IT WITH _____

NOTES FOR NEXT TIME_____

_____

_____

1. Who do you think are the best-looking male and female TV or movie stars? Why? (Listen for various standards used to determine beauty.)

2. Have you ever known anyone you would consider a "beautiful person" even though he or she didn't look like a movie star or model? Suppose we had a beauty contest that didn't take into account the shape of the body, physical features, hair style, clothing, or jewelry. How could you determine the winner? (The beauty of a "gentle and quiet spirit" should come shining through. [See verses 1-6.])

3. Do you think it's offensive to modern women to think in terms of being gentle and quiet? Why or why not?

4. Based on the parallel instructions given to men (vs. 7), do you think this part of the Bible is "sexist"? Explain. (Many women wouldn't like to be considered "weaker," though most women of the first century were probably not offended. Make sure no one misses the phrase "heirs with you" to show that women are just as entitled to the gifts of God as men are. God was promoting this kind of "equal rights" long before women themselves were.)

5. When I say "the Christian life," what do you think of? Living as a Christian may sound boring sometimes, but if we break it down into Olympic-type "events," it's pretty challenging. Try to recall a recent time when you knew the "thrill of victory" or the "agony of defeat" in these events from verses 8-12:

- Living in harmony with one another;
- Showing sympathy and love for each other;
- Demonstrating compassion and humility;
- Not repaying evil with evil, or insult with insult;
- Keeping your tongue from evil;
- Pursuing peace.

6. In five words or fewer, what do you think is the best way to avoid unnecessary hassles in life? What was Peter's advice (vss. 13, 14)? (If we're "eager to do good," most people will be glad not to bother us. Even if they don't, we should be strengthened by knowing God is pleased with us.)

7. Look at verses 15 and 16. Do you hope that people will ask you about being a Christian, or that they won't? Why?

8. How might you have to suffer as a Christian? If you weren't a Christian, how might you suffer? Which kind of suffering would you say is worse? Why? (Compare to verses 17-22. When Christians suffer, it's with the knowledge that God will eventually deliver them and reward them. But when people who don't know God suffer, it's without real hope or assurance—not to mention that many problems [rebellion, addictions, sexual problems, etc.] would not have such a powerful hold on them if they knew and obeyed God. Because Jesus first suffered and died, our own sufferings are not as severe as they could be.)

The reproducible sheet, "QuestionQuake," will challenge kids to be ready to answer questions about their faith. When they finish filling out answers individually, go through the questions as a group, letting everyone pitch in and answer more completely. Check for "gentleness and respect," as well as correctness, in answers. If some questions go unanswered, try to research (or have kids research) them for future meetings.

ＱUESTION ＱUAKE

"Always be prepared to give an answer to everyone who asks you to give the reason for the hope that you have" (I Peter 3:15).

"Say, you seem to have so much hope within you. What's the reason?"

What? You say nobody has asked you that question lately? Maybe you get a different kind of question—or would if a lot of other kids knew you were a Christian.

How would you respond to these?

1. "Do Christians believe every single thing in the Bible? I mean, do you really believe a virgin gave birth to Jesus? And that Jesus actually rose from the dead? How can you believe that?"

_____

2. "The one time I went to church, the preacher talked about 'following God's will.' How are you supposed to know what God wants you to do? Does He, like, talk to you? Or do you have visions? Or what?"

_____

3. "I know a lot of people who say they're Christians, but they go to all the same parties and do all the same stuff I do. You can't tell them from regular people. So why bother to call yourself a Christian?"

_____

4. "Why are there different kinds of Christians? You can't even agree with each other, so it's a little hard to believe that you know any more about things than the rest of us do."

_____

5. "I'm a science major, so I guess I can't be a Christian. You guys don't believe in evolution, or dinosaurs, or fossils, or any of that, do you?"

_____

6. "Actually, I've known some pretty neat people who said they were Christians. How would I go about doing that, if, you know, I decided I wanted to look into it?"

_____

7. "I hear that Christians believe that Jesus is going to come back to earth. Hey, wake up! It's been 2,000 years since He said that. Do *you* believe it's still going to happen?"

_____

I PETER 4

Suffering, Not Squashed

Christians may have to suffer at the hands of other people. But non-Christians often suffer *physically* from sin's effects—and *spiritually* because there's no other way to find God's favor. Since so much is at stake, Christians should concentrate more on loving others than on satisfying their own wants.

(Needed: Sheet with huge hole in it; newspapers or squirt guns)

Have a volunteer (a good sport) stand at the front of the room. Give other group members newspaper to wad up, or loaded squirt guns. Say to your volunteer so that everyone can hear: **Everybody's going to throw paper wads (or shoot squirt guns) at you for thirty seconds. But don't worry. I'll give you this sheet to protect yourself. All you have to do is hold it up.** Show a folded-up sheet you've brought. Your volunteer doesn't know that the sheet has a huge hole cut in the middle, which will make it nearly useless as a shield. Hand him or her the sheet just as you give the go signal for the onslaught to begin. Afterward, talk about how it feels to discover that you aren't protected from suffering. As this chapter shows, everyone—Christian and non-Christian—suffers.

DATE I USED THIS SESSION _____ GROUP I USED IT WITH _____

NOTES FOR NEXT TIME _____

_____

_____

1. Do you have any visible scars? Care to show them to us? How did you get them?

2. Who do you think suffers more: Christians or non-Christians? Why? (Christian kids may think non-Christian peers have it easier, but that persecuted Christians in other countries are worse off. Explain that Christians suffer their share of illnesses and other pain, as well as sometimes suffering for their faith. But non-Christians often suffer *physically* from sins—lust, drunkenness, etc—and always *spiritually* because Christ is the only way to find God's forgiveness.)

3. Have you ever had a physical experience that affected you in a spiritual way? Explain. (Examples: A serious illness that led to increased prayer; a "near miss" car accident that changed a person's priorities, etc.)

4. Sometimes physical pain and suffering can't be avoided, but we can choose how we respond to them. Jesus faced as much suffering as anyone—and He deserved none of the pain. What can we learn from His example (vss. 1, 2)? (We can "arm [our]selves" with the same attitude and determine to live for God no matter what physical things try to attract or affect us.)

5. When you choose not to do certain things, other people may think you're a little too straight, or even weird. What are some things you try to avoid because you're a Christian—things that other people actively pursue?

6. Why should you put up with being laughed at or misunderstood (vss. 3-6)? (We're accountable to God, not to people who are addicted to alcohol, sex, or something worse. They may seem to be "one up" on us now, but God's judgment will set the record straight.)

7. Have you ever tried to pray when you weren't totally "clear minded and self-controlled" (vs. 7)? What happened? (Examples: fell asleep, mind wandered, felt guilty, etc.)

8. Would you say being a Christian severely restricts your social life (vss. 8-10)? **Explain.** (It shouldn't, though it might mean we hang around with a different set of people and have different ways of partying. If we learn to "love each other deeply" and "offer hospitality . . . without grumbling," we should have some of the best social events around.)

9. If you said only things that you thought God might say (vs. 11), **how would it change your conversations in this group? At home? At school?** (Look for specific examples. Generally, conversations would be affirming, truthful, and gracious. We'd be a lot more careful about our words.)

10. When Jesus suffered (vss. 12-19), **do you think He endured it because He was thinking about the reward He would get, or simply because He loved humankind? Why?**

11. Next time you suffer unjustly, how could you endure it better than you may have done in the past?

The topic of suffering continues on the reproducible sheet, "It Only Hurts When I . . . " Have kids complete the sentences; then discuss. Then recall any scars that were shown at the beginning of the "Q&A" section. Explain: **We generally forget about our scars. They don't hurt, but they remind us of something painful that we've overcome. The sufferings we face now will soon be forgotten. Someday God will make sure of that as He surrounds us in His complete love. That's one reason to keep going now—even when it hurts.**

It only hurts when i...

Hello, and welcome to the Quick Studies Do-It-Yourself Psychiatry Correspondence Course. In this session we will deal with your attitude toward suffering. Just lie back on the couch and get comfortable. We'll begin a number of sentences, and you finish them with truthful answers.

1. Most people would suffer a lot less if they would only . . .

_____

2. If somebody really wants to hurt me, all he or she has to do is . . .

_____

3. The best way for me to recover from a painful situation is to . . .

_____

4. When I see other people suffering for something that's not their fault, I want to . . .

_____

5. When other people see me suffering, I wish they would . . .

_____

6. Whoever said, "No pain, no gain," is . . .

_____

7. If I weren't afraid of getting hurt, I think I might try . . .

_____

8. I think there is so much suffering in the world because . . .

_____

I PETER 5

Shepherds in Sheep's Clothing

People in roles of spiritual leadership should be willing servants rather than motivated by power, money, or other selfish reasons. And we should all show humility and learn to trust God rather than worrying. By standing firm in the faith, we can resist any attempts of the devil to mislead or destroy us.

Ask for up to eight volunteers. (If you don't have eight kids to play the roles, double up roles or bring in some adults to play them.) Volunteers will play the roles of young adults applying for a position as youth worker at your church; cut their instructions from the reproducible sheet, "The Case of the Evasive Applicant." Actors should keep their instructions secret. Other kids will act as the committee that interviews each of the candidates. Explain that the committee's task is to determine the best person for the job. Have the candidates apply one at a time to the committee. The committee may ask up to six questions of each applicant. Applicants must not lie, but interviewers are not allowed to ask directly why each person wants the job. See if your committee discovers the ulterior motives, or if some of the candidates can get through the interview without being discovered. Note the importance of pure motives for spiritual leaders—and others.

DATE I USED THIS SESSION _____ GROUP I USED IT WITH _____

NOTES FOR NEXT TIME _____

_____

_____

1. Do you know who the leaders are at our church? Do you know how they got to be leaders? (Discuss the structure of your church and the responsibilities of its leaders.)

2. Peter challenged elders to be shepherds over God's flock (vss. 1, 2). What words might he use today instead of "shepherds" and "flock"? (Managers over God's employees; directors of the cast and crew; spiritual coaches and players, etc.)

3. How might elders get caught up in a "power trip"? What should keep them humble and service-oriented (vss. 2-4)? (Even as shepherds, they're responsible to the "Chief Shepherd.")

4. Do you know older people who give you advice and/or help you mature spiritually? (Parents usually offer advice, though many young people don't listen too closely to parents. Discuss the importance of having spiritual "mentors" who take an interest and can provide wisdom during confusing times. Church elders will probably be happy to develop such a relationships with students who ask.)

5. Which of the following would you find it easiest to be submissive (vs. 5) to: (a) a man who had been a missionary to Africa for forty years; (b) a woman who had raised seven children; (c) your father; (d) your grandmother? Why? What might you be able to learn from each of these people?

6. What's the danger in "napping" (spiritually) for a while (vs. 8)? (Satan is always looking for a victim who is unprepared for his attacks.) When you're tempted, does it seem like you're being approached by a roaring lion or a silent panther? Why?

7. How could it help you "stand firm in the faith" (vs. 9) if you know that Christians all over the world are trying, too? In this group, do we tell each other enough about how we're struggling? What could we do about this?

8. Will self-control, alertness, and faith keep you from having to suffer (vss. 10, 11)? **Explain.** (No, but God teaches us to benefit from our suffering. As a result of such experiences, we become stronger and more steadfast.)

9. As Peter closes his letter, he writes of "Babylon" (vss. 12-14). Some think this was a reference to Rome, due to its evil reputation that would have put it in the same "class" as Babylon had been. What are some places today that you think might deserve the nickname "Babylon"?

10. How could members of this group show their love when they greet each other, if not with a kiss (vs. 14)?

(Needed: Metal garbage can or pie plate; matches or lighter)

Read verse 7 again. On a piece of paper, have group members identify current sources of concern that they're willing to "cast" God's way. When they finish, let them express aloud the cares they're willing to share with others. Then have them fold up their papers, which you'll collect. Without looking, pile the papers in a metal garbage can or pie plate. Say a short prayer to "transfer ownership" of these cares from the students to God. Then burn the sheets to symbolically show that kids no longer need to feel overburdened by these things—not if they really believe that God will take care of them.

THE CASE OF THE
EVASIVE APPLICANT

COMMITTEE

1. You want to be a youth worker because you think there's a lot of money in it, and you love money.

2. You want to be a youth worker because you think you'll have a lot of power over kids, and you love power.

3. You really want to be a pastor, not a youth worker. But you figure they're desperate to get a youth worker, and later you get can a promotion.

4. You don't really want to be a youth worker, but you're desperate for a job—any job.

5. You want to be a youth worker because you believe God can use you to bring teenagers closer to Him, and you really care about teenagers.

6. You want to be a youth worker because you like playing games and don't like to dress up when you go to work. You don't know much about the Bible, but figure you can fake it.

7. You want this job for only one reason: this church has lots of good-looking single people of the opposite sex, and you're hoping to get married someday.

8. You don't really like to be around kids. But you studied youth work at Bible college, so you figure you have to be a youth worker.

II PETER 1

Way to Grow

Christians should seek to develop the positive qualities that God makes possible for us (faith, goodness, knowledge, self-control, etc). These are all connected, and can be possessed "in increasing measure." We also need to have complete faith that prophecy and other Scripture are the inspired Word of God and not "cleverly invented stories."

(Needed: Fortune cookies)

As the meeting begins, explain that you want to discuss "future things," especially the futures of your group members. Hand out fortune cookies, one at a time, for each person to open and read. When everyone has shared his or her "fortune," ask: **Do you feel secure about your future now? Why? or why not? What other ways do people try to know what will happen in the future?** (Tabloid "predictions"; ouija boards; tarot cards; horoscopes, etc.) Explain that, as Christians, we are instructed not to participate in occultic methods of gaining future "knowledge" (as if we could trust them in the first place). But we have a much better way to be sure of future events—the Bible.

DATE I USED THIS SESSION _____ GROUP I USED IT WITH _____

NOTES FOR NEXT TIME _____

_____

_____

1. **When was the last time you felt really peaceful? What were you doing?** (People usually seek peace by trying to escape school and other stress, but Christians are invited to cast all their anxiety on God [I Peter 5:7], who provides abundant peace [vss. 1, 2]. Therefore, peace is possible even in the midst of everything else we have to cope with.)

2. **If you wanted to have a more peaceful life, or at least a more manageable one, what are three things you would need?** (After group members respond, discuss Peter's affirmation that God has given us all we need [vss. 3, 4]. Maybe we need to get closer to Him to find the things we're looking for.)

3. **Peter tells us to develop a number of other characteristics** (vss. 5-7). **Can you give an example of how Jesus showed each of the following qualities? Can you describe how a Christian you know has shown some of them?**

- **Goodness**   • **Knowledge (of spiritual things)**
- **Self-control**   • **Perseverance**
- **Godliness**   • **Brotherly kindness**
- **Love**

4. **Once you've developed these qualities, does that mean you've pretty much done all you need to do** (vss. 8, 9)? (Not at all. These characteristics can always be displayed "in increasing measure." In fact, the more we begin to understand these things, the more clearly we see how far we have to go.)

5. **What might *you* get out of developing those seven qualities?** (They'll help you keep from sinning, and you'll be richly welcomed into God's kingdom [vss. 10, 11]. Beyond that, our relationships should improve as we display things like kindness and love; we should find it easier to reach goals as we develop perseverance, etc.)

6. **With so many Christians around, why do you think we don't see more and better examples of self-control, godliness, kindness, etc.** (vss. 12-15)? (It's easy to forget how we're expected to act. Some of us need more frequent reminders than others.)

7. We always say we should let the Bible be our guide—for what's right and wrong, for what to expect in the future, and for most everything else in life. But how do we know it's any better than fortune cookies and other means of "prophecy" (vss. 16-18)? (The Bible contains first-person accounts from people who spent years with Jesus. Peter and others can attest to what they personally saw, heard, and experienced.)

8. The records of Jesus are one thing. But how about people "way back" in the Old Testament? How can we trust what they had to say (vss. 19-21)? (They spoke with the inspiration of God, through the Holy Spirit. The fact that the Old Testament prophets so accurately predicted the birth, death, and other events in the life of Christ should attest to their accuracy.)

9. Which of the following are hardest and easiest for you: (a) believing Bible prophecies about future events; (b) applying what the Bible says to real-life choices you have to make; (c) believing what the Bible says about Jesus; (d) finding time to read the Bible on your own? Explain.

(Needed: Guitar or other accompaniment [optional])

The reproducible sheet, "The Bone Song," deals with the list of qualities this chapter urges us to develop. Have kids sing the original "spiritual" and the II Peter 1:5-7 version if possible. Then have kids fill in the blanks. Discuss the results as group members are willing. Maybe a few volunteers will even be willing to sing their filled-in versions.

THE BONE SONG

Ever hear this song? It's an old "spiritual":

"The foot bone connected to the
  ankle bone,
The ankle bone connected to the
  shin bone,
The shin bone connected to the
  knee bone,
Now hear the word of the Lord.
The knee bone connected to the
  thigh bone,
The thigh bone connected to the
  hip bone,
The hip bone connected to the
  back bone,
Now hear the word of the Lord . . . "

Now read II Peter 1:5-7. OK. Here's how those verses might be sung to the tune of that "bone song":

"The faith is connected to the
  goodness,
The goodness connected to the
  knowledge,
The knowledge connected to the
  self-control,
Now hear the word of the Lord.
The self-control connects to
  perseverance,
Perseverance connected to
  godliness,
Godliness to brotherly kindness,
Now hear the word of the Lord."

Now here's another version of the same song. But your job is to think about the "bones" in II Peter 1:5-7 and fill in the blanks about yourself:

My faith is as strong as a _____ bone,
My goodness is as big as a _____ bone,
My Bible knowledge long as a _____ bone,
So here's what I need from the Lord:

_____

_____

_____

My self-control's as strong as a _____ bone,
I persevere as long as a _____ bone,
My godliness is big as a _____ bone,
So here's what I need from the Lord:

_____

_____

_____

My kindness is strong as a _____ bone,
My weakest bone is surely my _____ bone,
My strongest bone is surely my _____ bone,
So here's what I'll do for the Lord:

_____

_____

_____

II PETER 2

Liar, Your Pants Are on Fire

False prophets and false teachers will try to mislead us with creative lies. It may seem that such people are getting away with their deceit, but God is aware of everything and will severely judge them. In the meantime, He's more than able to protect His people, as He's done throughout history.

Begin telling a story, creating it as you go along. When you get to a crucial moment, pass the story-telling responsibility to another group member. He or she should pick up where you left off, advance the story line a little further, and then choose someone else to continue. Each person should try to make the story a little more unbelievable than the previous person. See how many people you can include before ending with, "and they all lived happily ever after." Then explain that while storytelling can be a lot of fun, we have to be very careful to separate made-up doctrines from the truth.

DATE I USED THIS SESSION _____ GROUP I USED IT WITH _____

NOTES FOR NEXT TIME _____

_____

_____

1. **What's the most recent lie someone told you? How do you feel when people lie to you? Why do you think some people lie as much as they do?** (To keep people from really getting to know them; to sound better or smarter than they really are; because it becomes a habit they can't break, etc.)

2. **Lying is never good, but it's even worse when you lie about God and the Bible. How do some people today who claim to be Christians lie about spiritual things, either through their words or their actions?** (Some say they are Christians, yet their actions never reflect that; some are hypocritical—pointing out the faults of others that are even worse in themselves; some spiritual leaders claim to be "of God" when they're really more concerned with power or money, etc.)

3. **How can a person make money from lying about spiritual things** (vss 1-3)? (By claiming that you need something extra [available only from the false teacher, of course]; by telling people what they want to hear; by claiming you need money to spread your false teaching; by "selling" forgiveness; by raising money to "protect" people from a made-up danger, etc.)

4. **We know God is loving and forgiving. Will He forgive the deception of these false religious leaders?** (God will forgive any sin if the person really repents. Yet the description of these people indicates that they have no remorse or genuine Christian concern. Because of their greed, they mislead some people directly and confuse others who are watching.)

5. **Peter makes it clear that the deceivers are deceived. They don't get caught right away, so they keep lying and think God doesn't see or care. What are some examples of how wrong they are** (vss. 4-9)? (God casting out the rebellious angels; the world during Noah's time; and the cities of Sodom and Gomorrah. In the latter two cases, the wicked people thought they had nothing to fear since they were in the majority, but it turned out they were "dead wrong.")

6. **What should people in the "godly minority" learn from these stories?** (God sees and rewards faithfulness—no matter how outnumbered we are or how powerful our opponents appear to be.)

7. **How do you feel when you read verses 10-19? How do you think Peter felt when he wrote this? If you set this passage to music, what would it sound like?**

8. **Do you think Peter is trying to scare his readers, scare the false teachers, or something else? Explain.** (This is at least a warning to both parties—to reject the false teachers and their ideas, and to abandon teaching them before it's too late.)

9. **The false leaders are compared to Balaam. Check his story in Numbers 22:21-38. How are today's false teachers like Balaam?** (Balaam [the one who was supposed to have spiritual insight] couldn't see an angel. God allowed a donkey to talk back to Balaam. Today some people claim to have "secret" knowledge, yet can't see the obvious truths of God.)

10. **Some of these people had apparently claimed to be Christians at one time** (vss. 20-22). **Do you know people who have said they were Christians, but who drifted back into their old way of life? Why do you think this happens to some people?**

The reproducible sheet, "Toxic Teachings," will give kids a chance to consider some false teachings making the rounds today. After kids write their warning labels, discuss. Some answers may involve the eternal results of following a teaching; encourage kids to think about the earthly results, too. For instance, believing that all religions are true could cause a person to think that religion is all in your head and should never be discussed, or that any behavior is OK with God, or that God is so lenient that He shouldn't be respected. Believing that animals and humans are the same could lead to treating people as if they were animals, or claiming that murder is OK because animals kill, too.

TOXIC TEACHINGS

Some people are teaching things these days that should have warning labels on them. Since there's no "Spiritual Surgeon General" to do that, maybe you could help out. On each of the following poisonous packages, write a label that explains what might happen to a person who accepts that teaching and tries to live by it.

"THE ONLY SIN IS NOT BEING TRUE TO YOURSELF."

"CHRISTIANITY HAS FAILED, AND MUST BE REPLACED."

"THE ONLY TRUE RELIGION IS TO BE AT PEACE WITH THE EARTH."

"HUMANS ARE NO DIFFERENT FROM ANIMALS."

"ALL RELIGIONS ARE EQUALLY TRUTHFUL AND ALL LEAD TO GOD."

"EACH OF US HAS GOD WITHIN US."

"GOD WOULD NEVER SEND ANYONE TO HELL."

"GOD WANTS EVERYONE TO HAVE LOTS OF MONEY."

II PETER 3

Coming Destructions

Because God doesn't *immediately* judge most wicked people, some think He's no threat to them. God is patiently waiting for anyone to come to Him who wishes to do so, but one day—suddenly—He will "stop the clock" to reward His faithful people and judge those who have continually rejected Him.

(Needed: Stopwatch; some "distractions")

Cover any clocks in your meeting place, and confiscate all watches. Explain that you will give a "go" signal, then you'll wait a while, and then you'll give a "stop" signal. After the "stop," kids should write down how much time they think passed between "go" and "stop." Then you'll compare it to the "official" time on the stopwatch. The first time, don't do anything between the signals. Wait thirty seconds or so and see how kids do. But then start making things more complicated. Wait longer periods of time as you carry on discussions, pop balloons unexpectedly, get up and play games, or whatever. You're likely to get a variety of guesses on time spans. Explain that God's perception of time is much different from ours, which causes confusion for some people.

DATE I USED THIS SESSION _____ GROUP I USED IT WITH _____

NOTES FOR NEXT TIME _____

_____

_____

1. Think about thinking for a moment. Let's suppose that your thoughts can be either wholesome, not wholesome, or neutral. What percentage of your thoughts would you say are "wholesome"? Why do you think so many of our thoughts are filled with worry, fear, confusion, and sin, rather than positive things? What can we do to try to raise the "wholesome" percentage?

2. What was Peter's suggestion for improving the quality of our thinking (vss. 1, 2)? (We should concentrate on the promises of Scripture.)

3. How does a person's opinion on the return of Jesus affect his or her thoughts (vss. 3, 4)? (Since it seems to be taking so long, some people convince themselves it's a myth. And if Jesus doesn't return, judgment doesn't take place, so why should it matter how they live? But those who believe wait in eager expectation and try to live to please Him.)

4. When God makes changes, they're usually big. He turned nothing into the whole universe. He sent the flood in Noah's time. And what will be His next big action concerning the earth (vss. 5-7)? (Heaven and earth as we know them will be destroyed and replaced [vs. 13].) **How do you feel about that? What won't you miss about the old earth?**

5. What can you say to people who ask why it's taking God so long to do anything about the mess that world is in (vss. 8, 9)? **God is getting blamed for a lot of the actions of sinful people. Isn't it time He did something?** (God is more patient than we are. He wants everyone to repent, and is allowing plenty of time for us to make that decision. Time is a human consideration. God is eternal, with no beginning or end. So we can't accurately accuse Him of being "slow" to act.)

6. When God acts, it will be "like a thief" (vs. 10). **What does this mean?** (Jesus' return will be sudden and unexpected.) **What do you think the people who accuse Him of taking too long to return will say when He does?** (Maybe that it was unfair of Him not to give more warning than He did. Critical people can usually find something to criticize.)

7. When people laugh at the idea that Jesus will return, should we laugh right back at them and say, "You'll be sorry" (see vss. 11-13)? **Explain.** (If God is patient while waiting for people to come to Him, we should be, too. There's nothing wrong with looking forward for better things to come, but that should inspire us to want to take others with us.)

8. Does believing that Jesus will return have an effect on the way you live? If so, how? If not, why not? (Discuss the importance of remaining spotless, blameless, and at peace with God [vs. 14].)

9. Peter knew some people were receiving Paul's letters and not making the effort to understand them. They distorted the letters to their own advantage (vss. 15-18). When you read something in the Bible that you don't understand, what do you do? How could you resolve your confusion?

Have a couple of kids perform the skit on the reproducible sheet, "Dwayne's World." If possible, encourage them to do their best impression of the "Wayne's World" characters from TV's *Saturday Night Live* and *Wayne's World: The Movie.* After the skit, discuss: **How did Dwayne and Gart feel about the return of Jesus? Are they like any people you know? What could you say to them? When you think about Jesus returning, how do you feel? What do you hope to accomplish for God before Jesus comes back?** Try to affirm kids as much as possible. The coming of Jesus can be a frightening concept to someone who doesn't understand, or who is uncertain of his or her spiritual status. Discuss the choices we must make, first in receiving Christ and then in how we live our lives.

Characters: Dwayne and Gart, two teenage hosts of their own cable-access TV show.

DWAYNE AND GART *(pretending to play guitars)*: Dwayne's World! Dwayne's World! Dwayne's World! Party time! Dwayne's World!

DWAYNE: Welcome to Dwayne's World. I'm your most excellent host, Dwayne.

GART: And I'm Gart. Party on, Dwayne!

DWAYNE: Party on, Gart. OK. Let's talk about prophecy.

GART: Prophecy? You mean like the future and stuff?

DWAYNE: I mean like the idea that Jesus will come back someday. OK. So what do you think?

GART: Oh, I think He's really coming back—NOT!

DWAYNE: OK. I think the eschatalogical ramifications of the theorized Second Coming are unclear. Scholars of the higher criticism school would postulate that this event is symbolic, rather than a watershed incident in real time. An orthodox interpretation requires a literal return.

GART: Huh?

DWAYNE: I was just kidding. OK. Let's talk about babes instead.

GART: Babes! Party on, Dwayne!

DWAYNE: Party on, Gart! OK. So, how many babes do you think we can meet between now and the aforementioned biblical return?

GART: Uh . . . I don't know. Why do we need to know that?

DWAYNE: Because, if it happens—and of course we hope it won't—that would be the end of . . .

DWAYNE AND GART *(pretending to play guitars)*: Dwayne's World! Dwayne's World! Party time! Dwayne's World!

I JOHN 1

Eyewitness News

The apostle John, an eyewitness to the life and events of Jesus, writes to let others know what he has seen and heard. If we symbolize our sin as darkness, he says, then God is pure light. Christians who walk in the light reflect God's love and fellowship. But some people claim to belong to God, yet continue to walk in darkness. Instead of hiding our sins, we should confess them and trust God to forgive us.

(Needed: Videotape, VCR, and TV; or catalogs)

Option One: Play a few minutes from a videotape—any drama or comedy involving people. Then have kids write their answers to eight or ten questions like these: **Who was the tallest person on the tape? How many people's shoes were visible? Who said the word "no" the most?** Then play back the tape to see which group member was the best eyewitness. *Option Two:* Pass out several mail-order catalogs. Let small groups examine them. Then have kids write their answers to eight or ten questions like these: **What was the most expensive item on page 3? Is shipping free? What town is the company located in?** Then check the catalogs to see which group member was the best eyewitness. Whichever option you choose, follow with a discussion of the importance of being observant—especially where spiritual things are concerned.

DATE I USED THIS SESSION _____ GROUP I USED IT WITH _____

NOTES FOR NEXT TIME _____

_____

_____

1. Have you ever witnessed an accident or a crime? What happened? Did anyone in authority want to know what you saw or heard? How did that make you feel? (Honored; afraid of making a mistake; worried that the person being testified against might find out, etc.)

2. The writer of this letter was John, who had been one of Jesus' original twelve disciples. He wrote the Gospel of John, too. What events do you think he wanted to testify about in this letter? (John was one of the three people who had been in Jesus' "inner circle." He'd heard Jesus' teachings and seen His miracles, but had also been there for "special" events such as the transfiguration and the prayer just before Jesus was arrested at Gethsemane. He also followed Jesus into the courts of the temple as they took Him away for trial.)

3. John was up against the Gnostics, false teachers who claimed that Jesus couldn't have been both divine and human. How does John blast their teaching as he opens his letter (vss. 1-4)? (He says he's seen and touched Jesus, which means Jesus must have been human. Yet he also says Jesus is "from the beginning," "the eternal life," and "was with the Father." John had no doubt that Jesus had stepped out of eternity to come to earth on the behalf of sinful humankind.)

4. John writes to make his "joy complete" (vs. 4). If John's joy wasn't complete, how could he be an authority about what Jesus can do in our lives? (Belonging to Christ *is* a joy. Yet the Good News about Jesus is not something to keep to yourself. John found joy in sharing that news with others.)

5. If you were a police officer, would you rather fight crime at night or during the day? Why? (More violent crime takes place at night; it's easier for criminals to sneak around then, and more dangerous for police officers.) How does this help explain the references to light and darkness in verses 5-7?

6. Do members of our group really have "fellowship with one another" (vs. 7)? What does the word "fellowship" mean to you?

7. Do you ever feel you're without sin (vs. 8)? Or are you more likely to feel sinful all the time? Explain.

8. If you keep struggling with the same sin over and over, how might confession help? (The more we confess to God, the more we can identify the sin and see how it affects us. We may begin to resist it at an earlier stage until we eventually overcome it.)

9. What verse in this chapter is most encouraging to you? Why?

The reproducible sheet, "Third Degree," will challenge group members to look at their lives *very* closely for sin that may be entrenched and unconfessed. When they finish the student sheet, assure them that God doesn't give us the "third degree" about our sins. He patiently waits for us to confess and repent. He may discipline us if we keep disobeying Him, but He does so out of love. Ask: **What's your mental image of God? How might that influence your willingness to confess to Him?** Spend some time letting kids silently confess sin to God and to receive His forgiveness.

THiRD Degree

It's like something out of a gangster movie. You slowly wake up from a groggy stupor and discover you have a massive headache. You're sitting in the most uncomfortable chair in the world, surrounded by three or four thugs who look and sound menacing. In front of you is a desk with a single item on it—a lamp. (It's not on.) The "gentlemen" explain to you that they are simply looking for a little "information" from you. They want to know what you've done wrong recently. Sitting here in a dim room with your head throbbing, what would you tell them?

(Write your answer here. Feel free to use a code—initials, maybe—for the things you've done wrong.)

_____

_____

_____

After you express your sentiments, they laugh in disbelief at your insufficient answer. They crowd around you, pressing in on every side. They turn on the overhead light, an uncovered bulb suspended on a cord. They ask you again, "What other things have you done wrong lately which you might want to confess?"

(Write your answer here. Feel free to use a code—initials, maybe—for the things you've done wrong.)

_____

_____

_____

In spite of the long list of wrongdoings that you've given them, they still aren't convinced that you've told them *everything*. They turn the high-intensity bulb on the desk straight into your face as they continue their questioning. And the last thing you think you see before the blinding light is one of them opening a package labeled "Bamboo Shoots—Fingernail Size." This might be your last opportunity to level with these guys. C'mon, *think*! Isn't there anything else you've done lately that you ought to confess?

(Write your answer here. Feel free to use a code—initials, maybe—for the things you've done wrong.)

_____

_____

I JOHN 2

Blinded in the Light

Though we try not to sin, sometimes we slip. When we do, Jesus isn't waiting to "catch us in the act." Rather, He's ready to act as our "defense attorney" before God. We confirm our love for Him by showing love to each other. If we don't watch out, we may start loving the things of the world, and we can be misled by "many antichrists" (vs. 18) who try to lead us astray.

(Needed: Blindfold and paper bag)

Blindfold a volunteer—someone who's good-natured and verbal. After blindfolding this person, put a paper bag over his or her head as well. Explain that the person should try to convince everyone that his or her vision is just fine. The others try to catch the person in the lie by asking questions that could confirm the inability to see: "What do you think of my new shoes?" "Would you rather go out with the person on my left or the person on my right?" The blindfolded person should bluff as confidently as possible. Later, refer to this activity when you discuss claiming to be "in the light," yet walking "in darkness" (vs. 9).

DATE I USED THIS SESSION _____ GROUP I USED IT WITH _____

NOTES FOR NEXT TIME_____

_____

_____

1. If I was arrested for a crime I didn't commit, how many of you would be willing to testify as a "character witness" at my trial? If I were a character witness at *your* trial, what would you want me to say?

2. We all know we're not supposed to sin, yet we do. When sin occurs, should we just forget about it and move on with our lives (vss. 1, 2)? **Explain.** (We should confess the sin—"plead guilty," so to speak. When we do, Jesus speaks up in our defense before God. Jesus has already paid for our sins.)

3. Does this mean that Jesus is telling His Father what good people we are, that we deserve to be spared? **Explain.** (We *aren't* good. It's Christ's righteousness that saves us, not ours.)

4. If forgiveness is so simple, what's wrong with doing whatever we want to do, asking God's forgiveness every night, and never worrying about our actions (vss. 3-6)? (If we remember what it cost Jesus to provide our forgiveness, we shouldn't develop such a callous attitude. God will forgive our sins, but we should never try to "manipulate" Him into forgiving us by intentionally sinning. Our obedience to God shows our love for Him.)

5. It's pretty easy to say we love God. How can we tell if someone is sincere about this (vss. 7-11)? (Real love for God is reflected in a person's relationships with other people. We don't truly love God if we don't show love for each other.)

6. Who do you find it hardest to show love for? Why? (Note that if we have problems with fellow Christians or family members, maybe the responsibility to change is more ours than theirs.)

7. Regardless of your age or gender, which of the "notes" in verses 12-14 could John have written to you? Why? What individuals and groups in our church deserve notes like these?

8. According to verse 17, "the world and its desires pass away," but in the meantime some of them look pretty tempting. What are some of the "worldly" things that crowd God's love out of the lives of teenagers today?

9. We hear a lot about the antichrist in connection with prophecy, but even in John's day there were "many antichrists" (vss. 18-23). Based on the definition given in verse 22, do you think any public figures today would classify as "antichrists"? Why?

10. John urges us to "see that what you have heard from the beginning remains in you" (vs. 24), and to "continue in Him" (vs. 28). Do you think it was easier to fall away from the faith in John's day, or today? What do you think it will be like to be a Christian twenty years from now? Why?

(Needed: Faintly smudged cloth)

Kids can apply the idea of "living in the light" with the reproducible sheet, "Sunblockers." When they finish, discuss. Then conduct an object lesson. With the lights dim, show everyone what seems to be a clean cloth. Then brighten the light a little at a time to reveal dirty streaks and smudges. Point out that unless we get nearer to the light of God, many of our own sins remain undetected. If we want to be more like Jesus, we need to be more willing to uncover and eliminate attitudes and actions we'd rather hide.

SUNBLOCKERS

The Bible says a lot about light. Jesus is the light of the world (John 8:12). God is the Father of the heavenly lights, who does not change like shifting shadows (James 1:17). And John tells us in I John 2:9 that "anyone who claims to be in the light but hates his brother is still in the darkness."

The problem is that even when we're "in the light," we sometimes try to block the "sun" of God from affecting us too much. For each of the following situations, circle the amount of "sunblock" that you'd want between you and the glaring light of God's truth (the higher the number, the less you'd be letting God affect you).

In the middle of a TV show you like, one of the characters starts using God's name as a joke.

0 Block   4 Block   8 Block   12 Block   16 Block   24 Block

Your youth leader asks for volunteers to go out and talk to strangers in the neighborhood about Jesus.

0 Block   4 Block   8 Block   12 Block   16 Block   24 Block

Your best friend is getting serious about someone who isn't a Christian, and asks your advice.

0 Block   4 Block   8 Block   12 Block   16 Block   24 Block

Your parents ask you for a little more help around the house.

0 Block   4 Block   8 Block   12 Block   16 Block   24 Block

You (or your girlfriend) are pregnant, and an abortion seems like the easiest way to deal with it.

0 Block   4 Block   8 Block   12 Block   16 Block   24 Block

Your pastor challenges everyone to help him by coming to a Sunday afternoon service at a local nursing home.

0 Block   4 Block   8 Block   12 Block   16 Block   24 Block

You have a chance to embarrass in front of the whole class a guy who's been calling you a humiliating nickname since you were in third grade.

0 Block   4 Block   8 Block   12 Block   16 Block   24 Block

A kid from a different race visits your youth group. Most of the members of your group ignore the person, apparently hoping he or she won't come back.

0 Block   4 Block   8 Block   12 Block   16 Block   24 Block

I JOHN 3

Love, Child

One result of God's great love for us is that He considers us His children. As children benefit by obeying and learning from their parents, we prosper as we imitate God. True children of God want to eliminate sin from their lives. The model for God's love was demonstrated by Jesus, who laid down His life for us. True love might require that we sacrifice ourselves and our possessions for others, too.

Select a good-natured person as an unsuspecting volunteer. Find a reason to have the person leave the room for a moment while you explain to the rest of the group what you want them to do. Then, when the person returns to the room, have everyone try to imitate the person—subtly, without being obvious. They should copy the person's posture and mannerisms, agree with his or her opinions, etc. See how long it takes the person to catch on. Then explain that as Christians, we're supposed to imitate God. We need to begin as soon as we can, because someday "we shall be like Him."

DATE I USED THIS SESSION _____ GROUP I USED IT WITH _____

NOTES FOR NEXT TIME _____

_____

_____

1. Most of us complain about our parents sometimes. But what are some benefits you've received from being your parents' kid? (Examples: Having food and a place to call home; someone to talk to; learning how to cook or fix a car; acceptance "as is.")

2. One of the greatest things about being a Christian is that we become children of God (vs. 1). What are some benefits you enjoy because you're a child of God? What are some of the responsibilities?

3. Have you ever had problems getting along with someone because his parents didn't much care for your parents, or vice versa? What happened? (This is also true about children of God and those who don't know Him [vs. 1]. We can't feel completely at home in a sinful world.)

4. What do you think people will be like in heaven? We don't know the specifics, but we're assured that we'll be like the Lord (vss. 2, 3) in some ways. Are you like the Lord now in any way? (We're created in His image; unlike animals, we have spiritual interests; to lesser degrees, we feel and express love, joy, etc.)

5. How can you tell the difference between the "children of God" and "children of the devil" (vss. 4-10)? (Those who are starting to conform to God's standards are His children. Those who willfully continue to sin aren't.) **Does this mean that anyone who sins isn't really a Christian? Explain.** (Most of us would agree that we aren't sinless. But if belonging to God hasn't gotten you started in obeying Him more and more, maybe you should reconsider your relationship with Him.)

6. Can you think of a time when you got into an argument with someone over something meaningless—such as where to go eat, what to do with some free time, etc.? Give some examples. (If we've had such arguments with those close to us, it shouldn't be surprising to discover bigger conflicts between those who pursue God's righteousness and others who live primarily for personal pleasure [vss. 11-15].)

7. All this emphasis on loving one another makes love sound really tough. But don't most of us enjoy being in love—sending valentines and receiving flowers and candy? Why wouldn't people *want* to love one another (vss. 16-20)? (The type of love we should display involves personal sacrifice and giving to others. It's a complete love directed toward all other people, not a specific romantic interest. It isn't achieved by "words or tongue," but with "actions.")

8. Would you say love is more a fact or a feeling (vss. 19-24)? Explain. (We certainly feel love for others sometimes. But other times love can be at work even when we don't feel it. Our unselfish and loving actions toward others are noticed by God, whether or not we feel anything because of them.)

9. On a scale of 1 (least) to 10 (most), how would you rate yourself when it comes to (a) showing romantic love to a boyfriend, girlfriend, or someone you'd like to have that kind of relationship with ; (b) showing God's love to some-one you don't particularly like; (c) showing love to par-ents and other family members?

10. What's the most creative way in which someone has shown that he or she loves you?

(Needed: Large sheets of paper; markers)

The reproducible sheet, "News and Comment," will help kids visualize ways to show love. When they finish, discuss. Then consider creating a large chart for the wall of your meeting place, modeled after the large "thermometers" frequently seen in fund-raising campaigns. Set a goal of, say, one hundred loving actions to reach the top. Have kids keep track of how many times they concretely show love to others each week until you reach the group goal. Reward yourselves when you reach the top.

NEWS & COMMENT

There are lots of ways to show love for people. Take a look at the news headlines on this page. After each, write how you could show love in these ways:

- **T** (time)—How could it be helpful to just spend time with the person(s) in need?
- **W** (words)—How could you *tell* the person(s) of your love?
- **A** (action)—How could you *show* the person(s) your love?
- **$** (money)—How could the person(s) use a gift of money or possessions?

Local Flood Victims Begin Cleanup

- **T**
- **W**
- **A**
- **$**

School Principal's Wife Dies of Cancer

- **T**
- **W**
- **A**
- **$**

HOMELESS SAXOPHONE PLAYER PLAYS FOR PENNIES IN PARK

- **T**
- **W**
- **A**
- **$**

TEEN ARRESTED FOR DRUNK DRIVING

- **T**
- **W**
- **A**
- **$**

I JOHN 4

Spirit Testers

The saying that "you can't believe everything you hear" is especially true in a spiritual context. We're instructed to "test the spirits" to make sure they're from God. Recognizing Jesus as God's Son is the sign we should look for. Also, God provides His people with His love and instructs us to do the same for each other.

(Needed: Names of professions written on slips of paper)

Before meeting, write an assortment of professions on separate slips of paper. Have a volunteer draw a slip and then try to convince the others that he or she belongs to that profession. For instance, one might draw a slip and say, "I'm a doctor" (or concert pianist, nuclear scientist, garbage collector, etc.). Other kids ask questions to try to disprove the person's claim: "How would you treat a concussion?" "At what level is cholesterol considered too high?" "What's your specialty, and what schools did you attend?" See who does the best job of "faking it." Then point out the importance of testing the *spiritual* claims of people who may not have a relationship with God.

DATE I USED THIS SESSION _____ GROUP I USED IT WITH _____

NOTES FOR NEXT TIME _____

_____

_____

1. How would you tell the difference between a counterfeit $10 bill and a real one? How do you feel when you discover someone has been "putting one over" on you?

2. We all get fooled from time to time. But when it comes to spiritual things, we need to be careful to "test the spirits" and not be deceived. What's the first test we should use to try to weed out "false prophets" (vss. 1-3)? (Anyone who doesn't acknowledge Jesus as being from God is not to be trusted.)

3. Why are so many people deceived by religious leaders who aren't teaching the truth (vss. 4-6)? (When people are told what they want to hear—which is often more soothing than what God wants them to hear—many will follow those leaders. God's people, however, should understand and follow those who speak for Him.)

4. What happens when conflicts arise over who's right—"them" or "us"? (We shouldn't waste a lot of time in pointless debates. Yet we can be sure that "the one who is in [us] is greater than the one who is in the world." We won't go wrong when we measure our beliefs by the Bible and stand by them.)

5. How else can you tell someone who really knows God from someone who just *says* so (vss. 7-9)? (A pattern of showing unselfish, unconditional love is a sign that God is in control of the person's life. God is the source of love.)

6. Since God first loved us, we're supposed to love others (vss. 10-12). Have you ever taken the first move in a relationship? What risks were you taking? What happened? What might have happened if God refused to take such a risk?

7. How do you feel about people who acknowledge that Jesus is God's Son (vs. 15), but who (a) speak a different language; (b) are from a different race; (c) worship in a way that seems weird to you; or (d) have a different list of "do's and don'ts" from yours? Which of these differences should be covered over by love?

8. Can you love someone you're afraid of? Explain. What does this have to do with loving God (vss. 16-18)? (We should always have the highest respect and reverence for God. But if we're always afraid that He's about to punish us, it's impossible to truly love Him. Our love for Him can only develop when we start realizing how much He loves and forgives us.)

9. It seems pretty easy to love someone who loves us as much as God does. But what about those who love us less (vss. 19-21)? (We must show love for our Christian brothers and sisters as well, which isn't nearly as easy.) Why do you think God tacked on this requirement? Why didn't He just say, "Love Me?" (The qualities of love listed in I Corinthians [patience, kindness, forgiveness, etc.] can be developed only as we work things out in imperfect relationships. God will never let us down, and we must learn to deal with—and love—people who do.)

Unless we truly believe that "the one who is in you is greater than the one who is in the world," it's hard to have the confidence to show love to others. The reproducible sheet, "Mystery Guests," will help kids consider what might be keeping them from loving certain people. After kids complete the sheet, discuss the questions at the bottom. Which of these reasons for not loving people could God have applied to *you* if He'd wanted to? (Answers: 2, 3, 5, 6, 7, 9.) Which of these reasons could God help you overcome if you let Him? (All of them.) Encourage kids to talk with you later if they aren't sure how to deal with difficult problems (such as abuse or feelings of inferiority) that keep them from loving others. You may want to refer kids with these problems to a counselor you trust.

Mystery Guests

What keeps you from loving everybody? Maybe a lot of things. If you feel rejected, for example, you might pass that rejection along to someone else instead of dealing with it. Or you may feel you can't love someone who has hurt you.

Try to think of at least six people you don't feel much love for—and what your reasons might be. Put the initials of these people in the blanks under the "mystery guests" on this page, according to your reasons for not loving them. You can put more than one set of initials in a blank if you like.

1. _____ I can't love this person because I'm jealous of him or her

2. _____ I can't love this person because he or she doesn't love me

3. _____ I can't love this person because he or she has rejected my love

4. _____ I can't love this person because I can't understand him or her

5. _____ I can't love this person because he or she has abused me

6. _____ I can't love this person because he or she is too far away

7. _____ I can't love this person because I have too many others to love

8. _____ I can't love this person because I don't like the way he or she looks

9. _____ I can't love this person because he or she makes fun of me

10. _____ I can't love this person because others might make fun of me

11. _____ I can't love this person because I don't feel good enough

12. _____ I can't love this person because
_____

NOW ASK YOURSELF:

Which of these reasons for not loving people could God have applied to *you* if He'd wanted to?

_____

Which of these reasons could God help you overcome if you let Him?

_____

I JOHN 5

Rules That Won't Ruin You

Showing love for God involves obeying His commands. It's not a burden to do that, because through obedience to God we overcome the struggles and limitations imposed by the world. We're also rewarded with eternal life and answered prayer. So we should eliminate any sin we discover in our lives and pray that others will do the same in theirs.

(Needed: Scissors; coins)

Form small groups (or use just one group if your have six kids or fewer). Have them play "The Pain-in-the-Neck Game" found on the reproducible sheet (give each small group a copy, along with a pair of scissors and a coin). This busy-work game can be played for fun if you set a time limit and declare the first group done to be the winner. But it's even more effective (and irritating) without the competition. Either way, discuss the game when it's done. Point out what a burden it was to follow the complicated, pointless directions. By contrast, God's commands are not burdensome—according to this chapter.

DATE I USED THIS SESSION _____ GROUP I USED IT WITH _____

NOTES FOR NEXT TIME _____

_____

_____

1. What do you have in your room that might show other people that you belong to a group or organization? (Examples: Trophies, ribbons, medals, musical instruments, lapel pins, certificates, uniforms, handbooks [such as a Boy Scout manual], etc.) **If you saw someone you didn't know with one of these objects identical to yours, what might you conclude?** (Probably that the person had similar interests and experiences.)

2. When people look at us, what should they see that would show that we're Christians (vss. 1, 2)? (Showing love to others is a sure sign that we love God.)

3. Is it pretty easy to obey the rules your parents set for you? Why? Which rules are hardest for you to obey? Why? Do you think any of them are completely unreasonable, or do you think there's a good reason for each one (at least, as far as your parents are concerned)?

4. Do you think God's "rules" are reasonable? Why? Why do you think so many people won't promise to do whatever God asks of them (vss. 3-5)? (Many people think God will "force" them to do things they hate to do. But the truth is that "His commands are not burdensome." In fact, our obedience to Him helps us to keep going in a confusing world.)

5. What is all this about "water and blood" (vss. 6-12)? (Many take this as a reference to Jesus' baptism and death. By insisting that the Son of God came "by blood," John may have been opposing the Gnostic heretics who said that Jesus became divine at His baptism but was only a man when He died.)

6. We're supposed to be confident when we ask God for things, but ask "according to His will" (vss. 13-15). How do you feel about that? What might you have to cross off your "request list" if you ask only for things that you think God wants you to have?

7. Should we care only about our own obedience, or should we measure how other people are doing as well (vs. 16)? **Explain.** (We should spend a lot more time on our own spiritual growth than we do "snooping" on others. But when we see a fellow Christian struggling in sin, we need to remember to pray for that person.)

8. **John refers to "a sin that leads to death"** (vss. 16, 17). **What do you think he means?** (Some people think this is a sin for which God brings about a swift and sudden physical punishment, as when Ananias and Sapphira lied to the Holy Spirit [Acts 5:1-11]. Others feel this phrase refers to the false teachers whose continual rejection of God's truth would eventually lead to spiritual death.)

9. **Look at verses 18. Is John saying that Christians can never be physically harmed? Explain.** (We are "safe" from the "evil one," which means that the devil can't take eternal life away from "anyone born of God." We can get physically hurt like anyone else.) **What do you want God to keep you safe from this week?**

Want to know a secret? It's shocking. You know how you hate those rules people put on you? The secret is, *If you just do what your parents and other people ask you to do, you'll get along great with them.* This is especially true of God's commands, which "are not burdensome" (I John 5:3). In fact, as we become obedient to God, we "overcome the world." As a group, brainstorm about a dozen of God's commands that relate to teenagers. Then brainstorm some ways in which these rules could actually keep us from hurting ourselves. (Examples: "No sex outside of marriage" would drastically cut the number of AIDS cases; "Don't let the sun go down on your anger" could prevent ulcers and broken friendships.)

THE PAIN IN THE NECK GAME

INSTRUCTIONS:

1. Cut out the shapes on this page to be used as game pieces. Give each person a shape. Each of you should write a name on your piece—not your own name, but the name of the person to your right.

2. Give all the pieces to the person with the longest hair. That person should redistribute each piece to the person to the left of the person whose name is on the piece.

3. Borrow a shoe from the person in your group whose last name starts with a letter that comes latest in the alphabet. Place all the pieces on the floor. The distance between pieces should be the length of the shoe.

4. Rearrange the pieces in alphabetical order, using the names written on them. But if today's date is an odd number, arrange them in reverse alphabetical order.

5. Have each person in your group touch each of the pieces, saying, "Oh, what a fun game," each time he or she touches a piece.

6. Flip a coin to decide which of the two oldest people in the group gets to turn all the pieces over so that the names are not visible.

7. Let each person pick a piece. Anyone who does not pick the one with his or her name on it must say, "Sorry, I picked the wrong one."

8. Flip a coin to decide which of the two youngest people in the group gets to turn the pieces over again.

9. Flip a coin to decide which of the two tallest people in the group gets to say three times, "Hey, the game is almost over."

10. Give all the pieces to the person in your group who hates this game the most (in case of a tie, split up the pieces).

When the Truth Doesn't Hurt

As we "walk in the truth," it brings joy to our spiritual overseers. This short letter is written as a reminder to love one another. John points out that some people want to deceive us, because they are not from God. If we tend to "run ahead" rather than follow God and what He has taught us, we lose sight of His will for our lives. We shouldn't welcome people who seek to teach spiritual falsehoods.

Before the session, copy and cut the cards from the reproducible sheet, "Word Weasels." Cut each card so that, for each obscure word, you'll have one slip with the real definition and two slips that say, "Make up a definition." Using three volunteers at a time, hand each a slip of paper with the same obscure word on it. Give volunteers a minute to create their definitions, and then have each present his or her definition to the group (one of which will be correct). Have other group members vote on the definition they believe to be the correct one. Use several sets of volunteers to see who comes up with the best phony definitions. Later, explain that a lot of people try to promote phony teachings about spiritual things. We must be careful to know the truth and recognize fakes when we hear them.

DATE I USED THIS SESSION _____ GROUP I USED IT WITH _____

NOTES FOR NEXT TIME _____

_____

_____

1. **What nonhuman things do people give names to?** (Boats; horses; B.B. King named his guitar Lucille; hurricanes are given names, etc.) **Why do you think we personalize objects in this way?** (In some cases, such as hurricanes, it's a way to tell one from another. In other cases, if something means a lot to us, we may give names to express that.)

2. **John addresses this letter to "the chosen lady and her children"** (vss. 1-3)**. This might be a specific person, though many feel John's referring to the church and the believers there. How might a group of believers be compared to a lady?** (It is the "bride" of Christ; its people should be inwardly beautiful and gentle, etc.)

3. **Do you ever call or write someone when you don't really have anything new to say? Why? What was the purpose of John's letter** (vss. 4, 5)**?** (It's a reminder to love one another. This isn't the only place in the Bible where we're told to do that, but we can stand to be reminded frequently.)

4. **Do you think** *you* **give anyone "great joy" when you're "walking in the truth"? Explain.** (Kids may not know how much it means to some older church members to see them in church and participating in Christian activities.)

5. **How do we show love to each other, and to God** (vs. 6)**?** (By obeying His commands.) **Does this seem like an unemotional kind of love? Explain.**

6. **What's the difference between an "antichrist"** (vs. 7) **and someone who just hasn't discovered the truth yet?** ("Antichrists" purposely deceive others with teachings contrary to Christianity. The false teachers during this time, for example, taught that the Son of God was a spirit who just *appeared* to be human.)

7. **What are some teachings you've heard recently that tend to deceive people?** (Examples: Reincarnation; "near-death" experiences that indicate there is no judgment after death, only bright lights and happy reunions, etc.)

8. What do you think it means, as you try to grow as a Christian, to "run ahead" (vss. 8, 9)? (Sometimes people want to skip "simple" teachings like loving each other and obeying God. They want to debate things like, "Can God make a rock so big even He can't lift it?" We need to let God lead us along as quickly as we're able to absorb His truth.)

9. Have you ever answered the door when a "cult" member came to visit? What did you do? Look at verses 10 and 11. Does this mean you should slam the door in the face of a cult member? Explain. (We shouldn't extend hospitality to false teachers in a way that would help them spread their teachings. But if we're really prepared, we might talk to them in a way that could help them see the truth.)

Have kids walk single file around and around the room as you say: **John tells us to "walk in obedience" and "walk in love." As I read off the following, show with your walk (limping, striding, struggling through mud, etc.) how you're walking in the following areas: (a) Loving your teachers as yourself;** (pause) **(b) praying for missionaries;** (pause) **(c) spending your money wisely;** (pause) **(d) working for a peaceful atmosphere at home.** Discuss if kids are willing, and spend time praying that kids won't "run ahead" or "fall behind" in their walks with God.

WORD WEASELS

---

marcel
(mar-SELL)
A curl made with
a curling iron.

marcel
(mar-SELL)
Make up a definition.

marcel
(mar-SELL)
Make up a definition.

---

kingcup
(KING-cup)
A buttercup.

kingcup
(KING-cup)
Make up a definition.

kingcup
(KING-cup)
Make up a definition.

---

flageolet
(flaj-uh-LAY)
A flute.

flageolet
(flaj-uh-LAY)
Make up a definition.

flageolet
(flaj-uh-LAY)
Make up a definition.

---

forb
(forb)
An herb other than grass.

forb
(forb)
Make up a definition.

forb
(forb)
Make up a definition.

---

defenestrate
(dee-FEN-uh-straight)
To throw out of a window.

defenestrate
(dee-FEN-uh-straight)
Make up a definition.

defenestrate
(dee-FEN-uh-straight)
Make up a definition.

---

lobbygow
(LOB-ee-gow)
An errand boy.

lobbygow
(LOB-ee-gow)
Make up a definition.

lobbygow
(LOB-ee-gow)
Make up a definition.

---

stiver
(STY-ver)
A coin from the
Netherlands.

stiver
(STY-ver)
Make up a definition.

stiver
(STY-ver)
Make up a definition.

---

hadal
(HAY-dull)
Having to do with parts
of the ocean below 6,000
meters.

hadal
(HAY-dull)
Make up a definition.

hadal
(HAY-dull)
Make up a definition.

---

gleek
(gleek)
To make a joke.

gleek
(gleek)
Make up a definition.

gleek
(gleek)
Make up a definition.

III JOHN

Gaius's Place

People who apply their Christian faith in practical ways are sources of encouragement—for the people they help and for Christians who happen to observe their loving actions. In contrast, self-seeking people hurt the spiritual growth of others. Our challenge is to observe and imitate what's good.

Before the meeting, cut apart the items (problems and their solutions) from a copy of the reproducible sheet, "First Aid Finders." Mix them up. When kids arrive, have everyone draw a slip without showing it to anyone else. (Make sure all slips drawn are matches for some other slip.) At your signal, each person should begin to pantomime the item on his or her slip in an effort to find the matching person ("poison" with "antidote," etc.). Confirm matches before allowing kids to say aloud what they've been trying to pantomime. This activity will introduce the need for Christians to notice problems (as Gaius did in this epistle) and to supply the solutions.

DATE I USED THIS SESSION _____ GROUP I USED IT WITH _____

NOTES FOR NEXT TIME _____

_____

_____

1. How do you decide who will be your friends and who won't? What determines your *best* friend(s)?

2. The Book of III John is a letter to one of John's friends, Gaius. What was the bond between them (vss. 1-4)? (Their commitment to Jesus. Apparently Gaius was someone John had helped to become a Christian, or perhaps was under John's authority as "elder" [vs. 1].)

3. When you write or call your friends, what are your most popular topics of conversation? Do you ever talk about the concerns of John and Gaius—health, spiritual growth, and faithfulness to God's truth? Why or why not?

4. During this period of church history, the Good News about Jesus was spread by volunteers who would travel and teach. Various Christians and churches would try to provide things like food and a place to sleep for these people. The evangelists who knew Gaius praised him (vss. 5-7) for helping in this way. What do you think other people would say about *your* hospitality skills?

5. Is hospitality only for people who have their own homes and apartments? How could you show hospitality to a traveling college choir that's going to sing at your church? (Encourage parents to let one or two choir members stay with you; ask around to help find them a place; help serve them food at the church; make them feel welcome by talking with them after the concert, etc.)

6. In contrast to Gaius was a guy named Diotrephes (vss. 9, 10). **What was his problem?** (His "love to be first" had apparently brought him into a position of power. He publicly opposed John's work, refused to support the traveling ministers, and could even expel people from church if they tried to oppose him.)

7. Do you know people who "love to be first"? How about people who "gossip maliciously" about others? Do you like to spend time with such people? What do you do if, for some reason, you can't avoid it and *have* to work with a person like this? (Discuss John's intention to confront Diotrephes and respond to his accusations.)

8. What are some ways that the people you know "imitate what is evil" (vs. 11)? Who are they imitating? (Friends, what they see on TV and in movies, parents, etc.)

9. In what ways do the people you know "imitate what is good"? (Compare responses between this question and the previous one, and see which is the longer list.)

10. Who in our group or church has recently had a positive influence on your life? Do you usually tell or thank people who have done something like this for you? What might keep you from doing so?

11. John says that anyone who does evil hasn't "seen God " (vs. 11). What does he mean? Have you ever seen God? (He was probably referring to the example of Jesus, which lets us see what God is like.)

12. John wanted to see his friend in person instead of just writing (vss. 13, 14). When would you rather "help" with a note or by sending money instead of seeing a needy person face to face? (Sometimes distance keeps us apart, but often Christians want to avoid people in nursing homes, hospitals, inner-city missions, etc. We need to remember the "hands-on" example of Jesus.)

As a group, plan to take on a project that enables you to either (a) show hospitality to others in your church or to people outside, or (b) come face to face with people in need. Suggestions for hospitality projects: Serve a meal for those over sixty-five in your church; invite another church's youth group to a lock-in; invite people in the neighborhood to a free car wash on a Saturday. Suggestions for face-to-face projects: offer help to an inner-city mission; distribute food at a food pantry; sing to residents of a nursing home.

FIRST AID FINDERS

FROSTBITTEN FINGERS	**MITTENS**
FLAT TIRE	**AIR PUMP**
POISON	**ANTIDOTE**
NOSEBLEED	**HANDKERCHIEF**
BROKEN ARM	**SPLINT**
HUNGER	**FOOD**
FATIGUE	**SLEEP**
HEADACHE	**ASPIRIN**
NEARSIGHTEDNESS	**GLASSES**
SCRAPED KNEE	**ADHESIVE BANDAGE**

JUDE

Spiritual Spies

Jude's warning to the first-century church is just as applicable to us today—watch out for people who claim to be Christians, yet who actually cause others to fall away from the faith through erroneous teachings. We need to identify such imposters and remain faithful to the truth.

(Needed: Chalk or masking tape)

Have kids huddle together while standing. Draw a circle around them on the floor using chalk or masking tape, as closely to their feet as possible. Explain that anyone who steps outside the circle will be "out"; but the purpose is to stay in, not to bump others out. What kids don't know is that a couple of kids, whom you've talked to before the session, will be trying to "eliminate" others without making it seem intentional. (They could be goofing off and "accidentally" knock someone out; they could clumsily trip and run into someone, etc.) Eventually the rest of the group may figure out what's going on. See if they try to toss your "spies" out of the ring. Later, explain that this is what some people have tried to do on a spiritual level—weasel their way into a group of Christians and see how many they can cause to stumble.

DATE I USED THIS SESSION _____ GROUP I USED IT WITH _____

NOTES FOR NEXT TIME _____

_____

_____

1. Have you ever been eager to do something, but then discovered that first you'd have to do a bunch of other things? (Wanted to play volleyball, but had to find a ball and put up a net; set out on a trip only to have car trouble; needed to write a term paper, but the computer wouldn't work, etc.) **How did you feel?**

2. Jude had a similar problem. He wanted to write about salvation, but discovered something else that needed addressing first. What prompted him to write his letter (vss. 1-4)? (The church was being threatened by "godless men" who were infiltrating God's people and denying Christian truth.)

3. Why does God let such things happen? Why doesn't He just wipe out anyone who opposes Him and tries to mislead others? (Anyone who refuses to repent of such behavior *will* be judged, but in God's perfect timing. In the meantime, Christians learn perseverance and discernment from dealing with such people.)

4. How can we be sure God will eventually judge people who stand against Him (vss. 4-7)? (Just look at history. Jude reminds us of [1] the Egyptians who enslaved the Israelites, [2] angels who rebelled against God, and [3] the cities of Sodom and Gomorrah. In each case, the faithful ones were separated from the others while God judged the wickedness of the group.)

5. Look at verse 8. How do people today "pollute their own bodies"? (This is probably a reference to sexual immorality. That's one way people pollute themselves today. Other examples might include smoking, drug use, etc.) **How do they "reject authority"?** (By refusing to submit to any church leaders; making up their own religions, etc.) **How do they "slander celestial beings"?** (This may have been a reference to opposing church leaders, but probably meant blasphemy against angels. Some people today "slander" God by claiming that He's cruel, powerless, or even dead.)

6. Jude says that godless people oppose what they don't understand (vs. 10). **What do you wish your non-Christian**

friends understood about Christianity? How could you help them understand?

7. Do any of the word pictures (shepherds, clouds, trees, waves, and stars) in verses 12 and 13 describe people today? How?

8. Look at verses 20 and 21. What did you do in the last month to (a) build up your faith; (b) pray as God's Spirit prompted you; (c) keep yourself in God's love; and (d) remind yourself that Jesus will return?

9. How would you feel if you'd had a hard week, and somebody said the words of verses 24 and 25 to you? How could you give the same message to someone else, but in your own words?

Read verses 22 and 23. Then have kids read and complete the reproducible sheet, "This Is a Job For . . . " (Possible answers: 1. Firefighter; 2. Nurse; 3. Toxic waste cleanup expert.) Discuss which of these helping roles kids feel most ready to take on. How can they better prepare themselves? What adults could help them with problems like those in the three cases? If possible, pray for friends and relatives who fall into the three categories from verses 22 and 23.

Be merciful to those who doubt . . .

People who have questions about God, the Bible, and the Christian life don't need someone to yell at them. They need a "nurse" to help them toward spiritual health.

. . . snatch others from the fire and save them . . .

People who are about to wander into a forest fire don't need someone to wave and say, "Have a nice time." They need a firefighter to stop them.

. . . to others show mercy, mixed with fear—hating even the clothing stained by corrupted flesh (Jude 22, 23).

People who have fallen into a toxic waste dump of sin need rescuing. But the "toxic waste cleanup experts" who do the rescuing need to protect themselves from falling into the dump, too.

In each of the following cases, would you need to be a nurse, a firefighter, or a toxic waste cleanup expert? Circle your answers.

CASE ONE:

Your younger sister has always loved slumber parties. Six months ago she went to a slumber party where the girls read their horoscopes from the back of a TV magazine. Your sister was so fascinated by the idea of "knowing" the future that she started reading her horoscope in the newspaper every day. Now the friend from the slumber party has told her there's an even "better" way to know the future—with a Ouija board controlled by "spirits." You've just heard about this, and the next slumber party is this Friday night.

CASE TWO:

Your best friend's grandmother died two weeks ago. Your friend and her grandmother were very close. Your friend is a Christian; but no one is sure about her grandmother, who hadn't gone to church in years. "I'm not sure I can believe all that stuff about Jesus being the only way to heaven," says your friend. "I mean, maybe my grandma wasn't a Christian, but she was a great person. How could God keep her out of heaven? Maybe everybody will be saved in the end."

CASE THREE:

A friend of yours hasn't been spending much time with you lately. When you see him at school, you ask what's up. He says, "Not much," and doesn't seem interested in your invitation to go to the next football game. That afternoon, as kids are getting ready to go home, you watch as your friend gets his stuff out of his locker. One of his notebooks falls on the floor, and a couple of pornographic magazines slip out. He sees you looking at him. Embarrassed, he puts the magazines back into the notebook and walks away.

REVELATION 1

Island Surprise

The apostle John, exiled on the island of Patmos, is given a "revelation" of God, describing things that are to come. John first sees Jesus, in all His glory, who tells him to write what he sees. So John begins his account and addresses it to seven churches in Asia.

(Needed: Magazine photos of people)

Spread out several magazine pictures of people. Some should be attractive; others should be intimidating. Then ask questions like these: **Which one[s] would you allow to stay overnight at your house? Which one[s] would you let borrow your tapes or CDs? Which would you give all your money to if they demanded, rather than asked nicely?** Point out that we take action for a number of reasons. Sometimes we act out of sacrifice because we want to. Other times, we act because we're scared not to. Our image of God helps determine how we respond to Him. If we take too much for granted in our relationship with Him, maybe we need to see Him in a different light. John did in this chapter.

DATE I USED THIS SESSION _____ GROUP I USED IT WITH _____

NOTES FOR NEXT TIME _____

_____

_____

1. Have you ever gotten punished for something at school? How did it feel? If you were in detention or grounded, how would you pass the time?

2. The apostle John is in "detention" as he writes Revelation. People with "dangerous" philosophies like his (Christianity) were sometimes exiled rather than imprisoned or executed. John was "doing time" on a small island named Patmos. What happened that kept him from getting too bored (vss. 1-3)? (He was shown a vision of the future to pass along to other Christians.)

3. John knew Jesus. He'd traveled, fished, and eaten with Him. As John begins his letter, is he describing the same "fishing buddy" he knew so well (vss. 4-8)? Explain. (In referring to Jesus, John uses terms such as "faithful witness," "firstborn from the dead," "ruler of the kings of the earth," "the Alpha and the Omega," and "the Almighty." John's view of Jesus had expanded.)

4. What does each of these terms (vss. 4-8) tell you about Jesus?

5. You'll get a lot more out of reading Revelation if you put yourself in John's place. So you're on an island, minding your own business, when you hear "a loud voice like a trumpet" (vss. 9-11). What's the first thought that goes through your mind?

6. Then you turn around to find out what's going on. What do you see (vss. 12-16)? How do you think you would respond at this point? (Compare to John's reaction described in verse 17.)

7. Are you ever scared of God—not because you've just done something wrong, but because you start thinking of how powerful and perfect He is? Or do you tend to take God for granted? (Because of Jesus' sacrificial death, we can "approach the throne of grace with confidence" [Hebrews 4:16], yet we should occasionally be "floored" [as John was] when we think of the extent of God's glory.)

8. Jesus told John, "Do not be afraid" (vs. 17). **If this were happening to you, do you think it would be possible to "not be afraid"? Explain.** (We may fear many things as we live for God, which is normal. Yet if we really believe that He's in control, we should never be scared into inaction. Jesus had a job for John, and regardless of his emotional state, he needed to get to work.)

9. Jesus' appearance was frightening, but His words were comforting (vss. 17, 18). **And He encouraged John to start writing. He even explained the meaning behind some of the mysterious symbols John had seen—the lampstands and the stars (vss. 19, 20). Why bother with symbols? Why not just come out and say what you mean?** (Maybe for some of the same reasons Jesus told parables: to hide the truth from enemies and the merely curious, and to say more than "straightforward" words could.)

10. **Can you think of anything that used to confuse you about God or the Bible, but became clear as you kept trying to learn?** (Explain that many things in Revelation will be confusing. It's important to gather as much of the clear meaning as we can, while trying to comprehend the symbolic parts.)

John learned that Jesus was there with him even when he'd been separated from the rest of the "normal" world. Jesus is with us in *our* hard times, too. The reproducible sheet, "Welcome to Patmos" will have kids draw from the attributes of Jesus to find strength to get through some of their current struggles. Let volunteers share a few of their responses. Spend some time in prayer, asking God for the things kids have determined they need.

Jesus' titles:

The Faithful Witness
If you can count on Jesus to be with you every minute this week, what positive difference could that make?

The Firstborn from the Dead
If you remember this week that you have eternal life (if you belong to Jesus), what positive difference could that make?

The Ruler of the Kings of the Earth
If Jesus can overrule any of the authorities in your life, what positive difference could that make this week?

The Almighty
If Jesus is more powerful than any problem you might have, what positive difference could that make?

The Living One
If you remember this week that being a Christian is about *this* life as well as the next, what positive difference could that make?

The Alpha and the Omega (the First and the Last)
If Jesus knows everything that's happened to you and everything that ever will, what positive difference could that make for you this week?

Holder of the Keys of Death and Hades
If you remember this week that Jesus has ultimately defeated the devil, what positive difference could that make for you?

REVELATION 2

Church Chat, Part 1

Jesus' message to four of the seven churches in Asia reveals a different profile in each case. The standard outline of each letter provides an image of Jesus, an acknowledgement of the things the church is doing right, a warning about sinful habits that may exist, and a challenge for the future.

(Needed: Coat hangers; string; tape; assorted small items; index cards)

Have teams assemble "wind chimes" from coat hangers, string, tape, and small items that you've brought (anything from pine cones to spark plugs to silverware). Then have teams test and judge each other's creations, Olympics-style, holding up cards with numbers between 0.0 and 10.0. After congratulating the winners, point out the connection to this chapter: The seven churches of Asia all started with the same "raw material" (the Gospel), but did different things with it. In His "letters," Jesus judges what they've done.

DATE I USED THIS SESSION _____ GROUP I USED IT WITH _____

NOTES FOR NEXT TIME _____

_____

_____

1. When you write someone a letter, do you have a regular format you follow? If you have good news and bad news to share, which do you give first? How about "mushy" stuff?

2. You don't often think of Jesus writing (or dictating) letters, but He did in this case. The churches He instructed John to send letters to weren't the biggest, or the most popular, or the best. Why do you think He would single out seven churches? (Some suggest they represent the changes that take place in the church through history, beginning with losing its first love [2:4] and eventually becoming lukewarm [3:16]. Whether or not this was the intent, they mention a variety of ways that churches [and people] respond to Jesus.)

3. Have you ever gotten praise that was followed by criticism? (Example: "You're doing a good job, but . . ." Or, "I really like you, but . . .") **How did it feel? How do you think the church in Ephesus felt?** (vss. 1-6)**?**

4. How might a youth group do good things today, even though it may have "forsaken [its] first love"? (Activities such as giving and service can be done out of habit or duty rather than genuine concern for obeying Jesus.)

5. How would you like to have been a member of the church in Smyrna (vss. 8-11)? Why?** (Its members were poor, persecuted, and being put to death. Yet Jesus had nothing bad to say about this church. Would your group members prefer such a "cutting edge" church, or a place that was safer and more comfortable?)

6. The church in Pergamum was commended for being faithful even "where Satan lives" (vss. 12, 13). What does that mean?** (Pergamum was the official center of emperor worship in Asia.) **Where in the world do you think it would be hardest to be a Christian today?**

7. How could the Pergamum church fight Satan but fall for false teachers (vss. 14-17)? How could the same happen to us?** (If we realize we're "fighting Satan," we're usually on our guard. But if we're hanging around with our friends, sometimes we go along with them without much thought. Or when an idea is labeled "satanic," we oppose it. Yet when the same thing is expressed as "one person's opinion," we might try to be open-minded enough to accept it.)

8. **The Church in Thyatira could truthfully say, "Hey, we're doing a lot better than we used to do"** (vs. 19). **That wasn't good enough for Jesus** (vss. 18-29). **How are you doing better this year in your relationship with God than you were last year? If you quit growing spiritually today, what problems might remain?**

9. **Some of Jesus' statements to these churches (and perhaps to us as well) seem quite harsh. Yet He ended every message with a promise. What's in store for us if we overcome the temptations and sins in our lives** (vss. 7, 11, 17, 26-29)**?** (Discuss each of these promises. Some are clear and others are a bit cryptic. Yet the point is clear: Faithful obedience to God will be rewarded in many ways.)

The reproducible sheet, "Letter #8," lets kids apply the outline of the letters of Revelation to your own group. When they finish, discuss what they've written and why. Then ask: **Do you think any of your comments are based on a personal, rather than a godly, perspective? Shouldn't Jesus just forgive the things we're doing wrong and let us get on with our lives?** (Not unless we confess, repent, and turn from our sins. Otherwise, we continue to hurt those who attend.) **On a scale of 1 (the worst group in the world) to 10 (the best), how do you think our group rates? Why?** Select one of the "needs improvement" areas that most agreed on; brainstorm ways to overcome the problem. If possible, assign kids to take specific follow-up action.

LETTER #8

Suppose Jesus had sent eight letters instead of seven in Revelation—and the eighth one was addressed to your youth group. Following the same kind of format, what do you think He might say?

Dear Youth Group at _____ (name of your church),

You need to remember some things about Me. I am the One who . . .

_____

_____

I've been watching you, and have seen you do the following things well . . .

_____

_____

But I've also seen you do some things that do not please Me. For example . . .

_____

_____

I want you to make the following improvements . . .

_____

_____

I must warn you that if you don't make these improvements, you will . . .

_____

_____

Stay faithful to me, because if you do . . .

_____

_____

   Love,
   Jesus

REVELATION 3

Church Chat, Part II

John concludes taking "dictation" as he passes along Jesus' comments to the last three of the seven churches: Sardis, Philadelphia, and Laodicea. Jesus' words to them are just as relevant to us today as He reminds us of our need to be alive for Him, rather than "dead" or "lukewarm." We need the same frequent reminder that we should overcome, because He could be coming soon.

Form pairs. Each pair will act out one of the following situations. The catch is that one person in each pair is supposed to act as if he or she is dead. The other must move the "dead" one around, make him or her appear to speak, etc., convincingly. The situations: Playing Ping-Pong; having a debate; practicing cheers as cheerleaders; singing a duet. Then take a vote to see who was most convincing. Refer to this when you discuss the church at Sardis, which had a reputation for being alive but was really dead.

DATE I USED THIS SESSION _____ GROUP I USED IT WITH _____

NOTES FOR NEXT TIME _____

_____

_____

1. What are some things you usually have to be told to do more than once before you get around to doing them? (Getting up in the morning; cleaning a room; household chores, etc.) **If you know you're going to have to do something anyway, why do you wait to be told four or five times, until someone else begins to get angry with you?** ("I'm busy," is a common excuse, but not usually a very accurate one.)

2. When we know what we're supposed to do as Christians, why is it we sometimes don't? (Frequently our own wants get in the way of what God wants us to do.)

3. Even churches sometimes need to be reminded to "shape up." What was the problem with the church in Sardis (vss. 1-6)? (Its reputation for life was false. Except for a few faithful people, the members were spiritually dead.) **Have you ever felt "dead" spiritually? How were you "resuscitated," or were you?**

4. "Philadelphia" means "brotherly love." Did the church there live up to its name (vss. 7-13)? Explain. (Yes, though with great difficulty. The people were pressured, yet they remained faithful to Jesus—and He let them know that He noticed.) **When you sing a song like "They'll Know We Are Christians by Our Love," do you feel it describes our group—or that we have a long way to go in that area?**

5. Can you think of a recent time when you were pressured by one or more non-Christians, yet remained faithful to God? (If so, point out that these group members might share in the reward of the Philadelphians [vss. 10-13].)

6. When you think of your overall service to Jesus, would you say you are very devoted, not at all devoted, or somewhere in the middle? Explain.

7. The Church in Laodicea was somewhere in the middle—"lukewarm," as Jesus put it. How did He feel about lukewarmness (vss. 14-18)? (It's the least desirable position to be in. If people coldly reject Jesus, they know where they stand, and perhaps He can call them to Himself at a later time through different circumstances. People who are "hot" are really obeying Jesus. But "lukewarm" people fool themselves. They call themselves Christians, seek comfort in the church, and expect the blessings of God—but don't make much of an effort to live for Him.)

8. **What promise does Jesus hold out for people who want to stop being lukewarm** (vss. 19-22)? (All they need do is "open the door" to enter a new and living relationship with Him.)

9. **Do you think it's a contradiction for Christ to say that He will "rebuke and discipline"** (vs. 19) **the people He** *loves*? **Explain.** (He knows what we don't—that going our own way rather than His will be harmful to us. So even though it's not fun to be rebuked or disciplined, it's better than any of the alternatives we might choose.)

10. **What do we get out of overcoming our sins and temptations** (vss. 5, 12, 21)? (Discuss each one, and the importance of seeing our lives from a long-range perspective rather than a short-term one.)

Use the reproducible sheet, "The Biography of Bobby Bland." You can do this as a "Mad Lib," with kids calling out the types of words and phrases you need before they know what the story is, or you can have each person fill out his or her own version. Then discuss: **Most of us don't want to be bland when it comes to things like food and music. Why do you think so many of us think it's "cool" to be lukewarm about following Jesus? How are you like Bobby Bland? How are you different?** Remind kids that Jesus is ready to welcome them into a new, warmed-up relationship with Him (vss. 19, 20).

The Biography of Bobby Bland

Bobby Bland was born in _____ (blandest place you can think of). The weather that day was _____ (blandest weather you can think of). When Bobby was born, his parents said, "He's so _____" (blandest adjective you can think of).

Young Bobby's favorite food was _____ (blandest food you can think of). His favorite TV show was _____ (blandest show you can think of). His favorite class was _____ (blandest subject you can think of). The music he listened to most was _____ (blandest music you can think of). His grade average was _____ (most average average you can think of).

When it came to church, Bobby was truly bland. He would dress in _____ (blandest color you can think of) clothes and sit in the pew with a _____ (blandest expression you can think of) expression on his face. When he sang the songs, it wasn't loudly or softly, but _____ (blandest way of singing you can think of).

When kids at school asked what he believed, Bobby would say, "_____ _____" (blandest statement of faith you can think of). When some kids wanted him to do something wrong, Bobby would _____ _____ (blandest reaction you can think of). When other kids wanted him to do something right, he would say, "I can't because I have to _____" (blandest activity you can think of).

When Bobby died, everybody said, "_____" (another bland reaction).

"I know your deeds, that you are neither cold nor hot. I wish you were either one or the other! So, because you are lukewarm—neither hot nor cold—I am about to spit you out of my mouth" (Revelation 3:15, 16).

REVELATION 4

So This Is Heaven

The apostle John is invited into heaven to witness supernatural proceedings. Among other things, he sees a central throne with someone sitting on it, 24 other thrones on which are elders, and four peculiar-looking creatures. The most common activity seems to be praising God.

(Needed: Prizes [optional])

Hand out copies of the reproducible sheet, "CodeCrackers." Have kids compete individually or in teams to figure out the answers. (Answers: 1. "Rolling in dough"; "A stitch in time"; "A bird in the hand"; "Once in a blue moon" (the key is the word that's "in" or inside another word, such as the word *rolling* in the word *dough*). 2. "KNIFE" is different because it's the only word on the list that has no rounded letters. 3. Bible, Sunday, church, study (each letter is before or after the correct one in the alphabet). After the contest, point out that parts of Revelation seem like a puzzle. And God has revealed previously "secret" information to give us better insight into life and what awaits us after death.

DATE I USED THIS SESSION _____ GROUP I USED IT WITH _____

NOTES FOR NEXT TIME _____

_____

_____

1. Have you ever gone through a door and stopped—either because you weren't where you thought you were, or because you weren't prepared for what you saw? (Examples: Walking into the wrong classroom; walking into a surprise birthday party; entering a room where the furniture has been rearranged, etc.) **How do you feel when you run into the unexpected?**

2. The Apostle John had a similar experience (vs. 1). **If you'd received the same invitation he had, and if you had a choice, would you go or not? Why?**

3. As you think of God sitting on His throne in heaven, what image do you have? (Examples: An old man with a beard; someone with lightning bolts in His hand; a judge at a bench, etc.) **How does this compare with John's description in verses 2 and 3?** (Rather than a specific description, John speaks more in terms of light and color [as might be reflected from precious stones].)

4. But God's throne wasn't the only one in heaven. **What else did John see** (vss. 4-6)? **What did he hear? What do you think these symbols represent?** (Explain that symbols are used throughout the Book of Revelation. Some are explained in the biblical text [see 1:20]. Some seem clear so that people have a strong consensus as to what they represent, and others cause people to be divided in their interpretations. We should stand firm on whatever points are clear, do what we can to understand the rest, and leave room for other interpretations of symbolic elements that aren't clear.)

5. It must have been difficult enough to John to figure out who the people were, but then he started seeing *creatures* like no one had ever seen before (vss. 6-8). Some suggest these creatures are angels. Others feel they represent the attributes of God, or images of Christ. **If the latter, what do you think is the significance of each one?**

6. If you were to try to describe God by using comparisons to four different animals, which four would you use? Explain.

7. What do you think it would take to be one of the 24 elders who were closest to the throne of God, and to these four creatures? What kinds of things do you think they did to earn the crowns they wore? With this in mind, what's important about what they did with their crowns (vss. 9-11)? (Even after we're rewarded for the things we do "for God," such things will pale in comparison to what He's done for us.)

8. If you really like someone, do you tell that person all the good things about him or her? Why or why not? Based on this chapter, do you think people praise God more on earth, or when they actually see Him? Why do you think that is?

Explain: **Several places in Scripture tell us about "crowns" we can have in heaven. Yet one of the first scenes in John's description of heaven is of the special group of elders laying their crowns before God's throne. After all the work they did, all the suffering they endured, they gladly offered their crowns to God. We shouldn't wait until we die to discover that God deserves our praise. Think of all He's given you. Have you been willing to "return" those things to Him in some way? What are three things you have—possessions, skills, interests, etc., that you could use for God in some way?** (Examples: A car that could be used to give people rides to retreats; a musical talent that could be used in youth group meetings.) **Before long we'll discover that crowns look a lot better at God's feet than they do on our heads.**

CODECRACKERS

1. What are these familiar phrases?

DOROLLINGUGH

TISTITCHME

HABIRDND

BLONCEUEMOON

2. Which word does not belong on this list?

PLATE	KNIFE	FORK	SPOON
CUP	GLASS	NAPKIN	DISH
UTENSIL	FOOD	DRINK	GOBLET
DESSERT	BOWL		

3. If each of these letters is just "one letter off," what are the words?

AHCMD   TTOEBX   DIVQBG   RUTEZ

REVELATION 5

The Lion Is a Lamb

John, continuing to witness heavenly events, is saddened to see God provide a scroll which, at first, no one is worthy to open. He is told that "the Lion of the tribe of Judah" is able to open the scroll, but when he looks he sees a Lamb instead. Yet as the Lamb takes the scroll, all the creatures in heaven began to sing praises to Him.

(Needed: Tape)

Prior to meeting, copy and cut the certificates from "Awards Time," the reproducible sheet. Post these on the walls around the room. When kids arrive, have them write their initials on the certificates for which they qualify. Then note how many qualified for each certificate. Do any kids challenge whether others are qualified? This should prepare the group to discuss the scroll that only the Lion/Lamb is qualified to open.

DATE I USED THIS SESSION _____ GROUP I USED IT WITH _____

NOTES FOR NEXT TIME _____

_____

_____

1. How do you feel when you're waiting for something big and exciting to happen? What if, at the last minute, someone demanded something impossible of you (a large amount of money, a college degree, etc.) **before that event could take place? Then how would you feel?**

2. What similar situation did John witness as he was allowed to view proceedings in heaven (vss. 1-3)? (God was providing a mysterious scroll with seven seals, yet no one was worthy of opening it.)

3. How would you have felt in John's place? How did he feel (vs. 4)**? Why?** (He "wept and wept." It must have seemed like receiving a valuable gift, but being incapable of finding out how to open it to see what was inside.)

4. Who was finally declared able to open the scroll (vs. 5)**? Why?** ("The Lion of the tribe of Judah," because He "has triumphed." This title is from Genesis 49:8-10.)

5. But instead of a Lion, John saw a Lamb (vs. 6)**. What was a little different about this Lamb?** (He looked like He had previously been killed, and He had seven horns and seven eyes. [Horns are generally a symbol of strength.])

6. Sheep aren't usually animals that command a lot of respect. Was that true of this "Lamb" (vss. 7, 8)**?** (This "Lamb" was held in highest regard by the elders who surrounded the throne and the four creatures [introduced in chapter 4].)

7. In describing this scene around God's throne, John has not mentioned a lot of people so far—just the 24 elders. Yet in what way were other people represented there? (Each elder held a bowl of incense, which represented "the prayers of the saints.") **Have you ever felt God wasn't hearing your prayers? What does this "incense" tell you about that?** (God does hear and value our prayers, which are like sweet-smelling incense to Him.)

8. As the groups in heaven began to sing praises to the Lamb, they revealed things about Him. What do we learn

from the elders (vss. 9, 10)? (His blood was shed so He could "purchase men for God," and as a result they would serve God and reign on the earth.) **What do we learn from the angels** (vss. 11, 12)? (The Lamb was slain, and has received power, wealth, wisdom, strength, honor, glory, and praise.)

9. The praise came from "every creature in heaven and on earth and under the earth and on the sea, and all that is in them" (vss. 13, 14). Whom or what would you be most surprised to see praising God? Why?

10. It seems that someday praise will be an important part of your life. How much practice are you getting? Explain.

11. Jesus' name is never mentioned in this chapter, so how can we be sure that's who the passage refers to? (The references are unmistakable: the lion of Judah, the connection to David, the Lamb who was slain, and His right to receive praise from both people and angels.)

12. Why do you think the image of Jesus as a Lamb continues in heaven? His sacrifice is complete, so wouldn't the Lion image be a better fit? (It's because of His sacrifice that He's worthy to open the scroll. In later chapters, as the judgment of God is revealed, it becomes obvious that judgment is based on the refusal of people to respond to the sacrifice Jesus made for them.)

Say: **This chapter opens with weeping and ends with "a new song" of praise. Here's your chance to write a song of your own that praises the Lord Jesus. A short, little chorus will do—or even a bold fanfare with no words. Whatever you do, the goal should be to praise God with it. Start with what you want to communicate. You can be sure that God will appreciate it (no matter what anyone else might say).** (If you think this will be too intimidating for some kids, let them work in groups.) When they finish, let volunteers teach their songs to the group.

Awards Time

This is to certify that

_____

has completed one year of perfect
attendance in our group.

By these presents be it known that

_____

has uttered no rude or sullen words to
his or her parents this week.

This is to certify that

_____

told someone about Jesus today.

Hear ye! Hear ye!

_____

has been kind to animals all year.

This certificate goes to

_____

for contributing more than a dollar to
the offering this week.

We hereby recognize that

_____

has never started a fistfight.

In appreciation to

_____

for memorizing more than 12 Bible
verses this year.

This is to certify that

_____

has not committed a single sin today.

REVELATION 6

The Beginning Of the End

The Lamb in heaven begins to open the scroll that has seven seals (which He was given in chapter 5). With each seal that is opened, a catastrophic event takes place. As the judgment of God approaches, the world will be beset by conquest, war, famine, death, and earthquakes, among other things. [NOTE: From this chapter on, these sessions are worded in a way that assumes that most of the events take place in the future. There are some who hold that the events of chapters 6-18 have already taken place throughout history. If you hold the latter view, be ready to adapt questions and answers accordingly.]

(Needed: Markers, tape, and a large sheet of newsprint)

Fasten a large sheet of newsprint to one wall. Hand out markers and ask group members to create a "disaster mural." (Make sure the markers won't leak through to the wall.) Kids should draw whatever they consider to be disasters: floods, tidal waves, earthquakes, avalanches, famines, hurricanes, killer bees, getting turned down for a date, etc. Explain that there is a difference between these "natural" disasters and the judgments of God that will come during the end times, which will be "supernatural" disasters.

DATE I USED THIS SESSION _____ GROUP I USED IT WITH _____

NOTES FOR NEXT TIME _____

_____

_____

1. Have you ever lived through a natural disaster—flood, tornado, earthquake, etc.? How did this event affect your daily routine? How did it cause people to relate to each other? (When people are threatened with something that has the potential to kill or hurt them, they usually put personal differences behind them.)

2. Whatever people have experienced so far, the worst is yet to come. As the end approaches, God will allow a level of destruction that has never been seen before. Do you think it was right for the Apostle John to "spy" on these things and pass the signs on to us? (Yes, because that's why he was there. He wasn't spying. He was specifically invited to watch what was happening here [vss. 1, 3, 5, and 7].)

3. What was one of the first signs he witnessed (vss. 1, 2)? What does it mean? (The white horse, which represents conquest. [Some people try to be more specific by identifying the rider. One group argues that he is the antichrist; another group believes the rider might be Jesus.])

4. What happened when the second seal was opened (vss. 3-4)? (A rider on a red horse appeared.) What do you think this one represents? (Apparently war, based on the actions of the rider.)

5. The third seal revealed a black horse. With what is this horse and rider associated (vss. 5, 6)? Why? (The indication is famine, based on the exorbitant costs of food.)

6. Do you think the riders of the horses are in control of their actions and what happens on earth? Explain. (We get a clue in verse 6 where one of the heavenly creatures places limits on the extent of the rider's influence. ["Do not damage the oil and the wine."])

7. Seal #4 is a bit more clear (vss. 7, 8). Who is the rider, and how does he accomplish his destructive mission? (The rider is Death. A fourth of the people will die by weapons, famine, plague, and even wild beasts.)

8. The horses and riders linked to the first four seals are frequently referred to as the Four Horsemen of the Apocalypse. The "horsemen" are limited to four, but the opening of the seals continues. The fifth seal reveals a different perspective of what is happening on earth. **What did John see (vss. 9-11)?** (He saw the souls of people who had been killed because of their belief in Jesus. They were calling for justice and judgment.)

9. The request of the martyrs seems reasonable; why didn't God answer their prayers? (He was waiting. He knew other people were still going to die for Him. But in the meantime, He provided each of the faithful martyrs with a white robe, symbolic of their new status of purity and glory.)

10. If God knew that more faithful people were going to die, why do you think He waited instead of acting sooner? (God wants all people to be saved [I Timothy 2:3, 4; II Peter 3:9]. He isn't waiting for more of His people to be killed, but for more who aren't His to turn to Him.)

11. When the sixth seal is opened, it triggers other disasters. Do you think people will connect these things to God, or will they come up with more "scientific" explanations (vss. 13-17)? (By this time, even many of the "greatest" people on earth will figure out that God is not pleased.)

12. It shouldn't take disasters to get a Christian's attention. What are some "smaller" things you see from time to time that remind you to stop and thank God? (A beautiful rainbow or sunset; a loving action by a parent; "just the right" Bible verse at "just the right" time, etc.)

The reproducible sheet, "Don't Say I Didn't Warn You," will help kids see that God has already given us some "signs" that can warn us when we're headed for trouble. Let volunteers display their signs. Ask: **Do you pay attention to biblical warnings, or do you keep heading down the road until you "hit" something physically or emotionally? What could help you pay more attention to such signs before you get too far down the road?** Encourage kids to watch for signs like these as well as for those heralding the end of the age.

DON'T SAY I DIDN'T WARN YOU!

God has put up a lot of warning signs—not just about disasters at the end of the world, but about disasters that could wreck our personal worlds. He sees us headed into something that might hurt us spiritually. So He puts obstacles in our paths to slow us down. But we find a way around them. He provides people to deal with us truthfully, but we ignore them. If he spelled out a personal warning using clouds to write on the sky, we'd call it a coincidence.

What "signs" has God posted on the way to each of the following disastrous destinations? These can be Bible quotations, physical symptoms, costs, advice other Christians might give you, etc. We've supplied a few for you. See how you do on the rest.

REVELATION 7

A Tamperproof Seal

Though massive destruction is in store for the earth, God is in control. Before He allows the devastating forces to be unleashed, He ensures that many of His people are "sealed." And even though the "great tribulation" is at hand, the number of people who turn to God during this time compose "a great multitude that no one could count, from every nation, tribe, people and language" (vs. 9).

(Needed: Plans for a bowling trip, or a plastic toy bowling set)

Consider going bowling just before this session. If going to a bowling alley isn't possible, bring a toy bowling set (the inexpensive plastic kind sold in many toy stores) and roll a few frames. The effort made to knock down all ten pins with every ball, and the frustration of not being able to, make a good illustration. Point out that God will never allow Satan's evil forces to "bowl a 300 game." Even in the midst of the worst possible persecution, God will be sure that a "remnant" of people will remain standing (like those bowling pins) to be His witnesses in a world that has turned away from Him.

DATE I USED THIS SESSION _____ GROUP I USED IT WITH _____

NOTES FOR NEXT TIME _____

_____

_____

1. Can you think of a time when you were "saved by the bell"—when you were rescued at the last minute from being harmed, embarrassed, or otherwise hurt?

2. The trouble that hits the earth during the last days will be of a magnitude that people have never experienced (Matthew 24:21). **Yet even as the world faces this final cataclysm, how does God ensure that His people aren't completely destroyed** (vss. 1-3)? (They receive "seals" [in much the same way that letters from a king were sealed to show they were authentic and to be protected].)

3. Who are the 144,000 (vss. 4-8)? (Some feel they are literally a faithful Jewish remnant; others take the number as a symbol of all faithful believers who live then.) **If you're a Christian, do you feel like you're part of a remnant (a small minority), or in the majority? Why?**

4. So far, John's description of heaven has not included great numbers of people. But that's about to change. **What's his next vision** (vss. 9, 10)? (More people than anyone could count, gathered around the throne [in front of both God and His Son] and offering praise for their salvation.) **What response did these people get from their heavenly counterparts** (vss. 11, 12)? (The angels, elders, and living creatures [introduced in chapters 4 and 5] all joined them in worship. They seemed as overjoyed over the salvation of these people as the people were themselves.)

5. How many people do you think will be in heaven? How many would you like to bring with you through sharing your faith?

6. At this point, one of the 24 elders turned to John and asked where these people came from (vs. 13). **If you'd been in John's place, how would you have replied?** (John respectfully turned the question back to the elder to answer. The elder explained that these people had come out of "the great tribulation" (vs. 14). They probably had experienced persecution and death because they were believers.)

7. Doesn't God care what happens to His people? If so, why are there so many people here who apparently died for their faith? (We live in a sinful world. Sometimes we experience the results of that sin. God has the power to intervene, but doesn't always do so. We're given the power of the Holy Spirit as we face trouble, but that doesn't prevent Christians from being persecuted and even killed. This will become more true as the world in general turns away from God to follow a leader committed to Satan.)

8. When we face tough situations as Christians, what should we always keep in mind (vss. 14-17)? (God rewards faithfulness. The martyrs of the tribulation, for example, receive the privilege of serving "before the throne of God" so God can wipe away every tear from their eyes. No longer will they suffer hunger, thirst, scorching heat, or anything that bothered them before.)

9. Do you really believe the rewards in heaven are worth suffering here on earth? Can you put up with persecution (or just missing out on some "fun") for "a little while" until you see God face to face? How do you feel about the persecution you may face?

The reproducible sheet, "No More Tears," will help kids see what an incredible accomplishment it will be for God to wipe away the tears of His people in heaven (vs. 17). If kids are willing, discuss the reasons why they have cried (or have felt like crying) in the last year or so. Remind them that for now, crying is sometimes exactly the right response—to our own pain and to the pain of others. Then spend some time planning a social event that will help counteract some of the negative experiences kids face. Christianity doesn't *always* require tears or sadness, even in this life.

No More TEARS

Here are some ways to stop crying—more or less. Have you tried any of them? Have you seen others try them? Do any of them really work? Check off your answers below.

I'VE TRIED IT	SAW OTHERS TRY IT	IT WORKS	
❑	❑	❑	Use gentle baby shampoo
❑	❑	❑	Put microscopic corks in your tear ducts
❑	❑	❑	Don't watch any sad movies or TV shows
❑	❑	❑	Dull the pain of life by drinking alcohol
❑	❑	❑	Dry yourself up with antihistimines
❑	❑	❑	Refuse to slice onions
❑	❑	❑	Think of life as a big joke
❑	❑	❑	Watch the comedy cable channel 24 hours a day
❑	❑	❑	Convince yourself that big guys (or girls) don't cry
❑	❑	❑	Don't watch the TV news
❑	❑	❑	Don't listen to any sad songs
❑	❑	❑	Stay in a fog with drugs
❑	❑	❑	Don't read the newspaper
❑	❑	❑	Avoid all relationships
❑	❑	❑	Have lots of relationships
❑	❑	❑	Never think about death
❑	❑	❑	Hurt people before they can hurt you
❑	❑	❑	Stay away from needy people
❑	❑	❑	Suppress all emotions through willpower
❑	❑	❑	Pretend that Christians are never sad
❑	❑	❑	Avoid all germs so you won't get any painful diseases
❑	❑	❑	Live in a padded room so you'll never get injured
❑	❑	❑	Other _____
❑	❑	❑	Other _____

"And God will wipe away every tear from their eyes" (Revelation 7:17).

REVELATION 8

Calm before The Storm

The opening of the scroll's seventh seal results in a hushed silence for about half an hour, after which begin the series of trumpet judgments. During this sequence, large areas of the earth are destroyed—trees, grass, oceans, and fresh water. Animals and people die as well.

(Needed: Stopwatch)

See how well your group can do at achieving total silence. Use a stopwatch and time yourselves. Whenever anyone talks, giggles, coughs, sneezes, causes chairs to squeak, etc., start over. Soon you should be able to discern a level of sounds that you don't usually notice: furnaces or air conditioners kicking on, the wind outside, creaks in the building, etc. If your group can approach five minutes' worth of complete silence, they're doing well. Compare this to the half hour of heavenly silence in this chapter.

DATE I USED THIS SESSION _____ GROUP I USED IT WITH _____

NOTES FOR NEXT TIME _____

_____

_____

1. What percentage of the time while you're awake would you say is spent in silence—no music, TV in the background, conversation, or anything else making noise? Are you comfortable with silence, or do you prefer to have something going on around you? Why?

2. Have you ever been stunned into silence? Has some event or piece of news so shocked you that you couldn't even say anything?

3. John has been witnessing some incredible future events in heaven. But as the seventh seal is opened, everyone in heaven is quiet for about half an hour (vs. 1). Why? (Apparently because what is to come is more intense than anything that's taken place so far.)

4. In the Old Testament Tabernacle, a "censer" (shaped something like a saucepan) was used to carry coals from the bronze altar outside to the altar of incense inside. Then incense would be added to the coals, and smoke would rise as a symbol of the person's prayers ascending to God. With this in mind, what's the meaning of the angel's actions described in verses 3-5? ("The prayers of the saints" are offered on a heavenly altar in God's presence. Perhaps the time has not been right, prior to this moment, for God to act on these prayers. [If, for instance, we have ever prayed for God to triumph over evil and eliminate wickedness, maybe those prayers will be "on hold" until this time.])

5. The angel throws the fiery censer to earth (vs. 5). If someone were to set on fire all the prayers you've prayed for God's will to be done, would the result be (a) a bonfire, (b) a campfire, (c) a little smoke, or (d) something else? Explain.

6. Seven other angels are called on to deliver the trumpet judgments (vs. 2). What might God use to accomplish the effects described in verses 6 and 7? (Speculations: comets; nuclear war; meteor showers; asteroids; some other divine means of showering the earth with "hail and fire.")

7. With the sounding of the second trumpet, "something like a huge mountain, all ablaze, was thrown into the sea" (vss. 8, 9). **Do you think anything like this has ever happened? Explain.** (Apparently not, since in this case it destroys a third of all ships and sea life. This is no ordinary meteorite or satellite falling out of orbit.)

8. Look at verses 10 and 11. **Why is the star's name mentioned?** ("Wormwood" is a bitter tasting plant, symbolic of sorrow.)

9. The fourth trumpet judgment dims the light of the sun, moon, and stars by a third (vs. 12). **How would you feel if suddenly the days and nights became a lot darker?**

10. **What would impress you most if you were one of the following people reading Revelation 8: (a) the Secretary of the Navy; (b) a tribal "witch doctor"; (c) an astronomer; (d) an environmental expert; (d) someone who believed that God was a lot like Santa Claus?**

In this chapter the martyred saints' prayers for justice are heard and acted on. The reproducible sheet, "A Cry for Justice," brings home the idea of praying for justice. Have kids fill out the sheet; then discuss. Kids' prayers may vary widely, depending on their ideas of justice. Encourage them to consider tempering justice with mercy as needed. Ask: **Are you used to praying for justice? Do you pray that justice will be done for other people, or just for yourself? What injustice bothers you most?** Try to include some silent prayer, too.

A CRY FOR JUSTICE

In Revelation 6, Christians who have been killed for their faith cry out for justice. In Revelation 8, God acts on their prayers in an earth-shaking way.

Do you ever pray for justice—that God will stop evil and make things the way they ought to be? Your request may not be answered right away, or in the way you expect. But if you want justice to be done, what short prayer could you pray about each of the following?

The Ku Klux Klan
"_____"

Your first period teacher
"_____"

The nearest "adult" bookstore
"_____"

A drunk driver who killed someone from your school
"_____"

Your father (or mother's) boss at work
"_____"

Doctors who perform abortions
"_____"

A child who is born with AIDS
"_____"

Illegal immigrants trying to enter the U.S.
"_____"

A girl who was attacked by gang members
"_____"

A government that jails people for becoming Christians
"_____"

A serial killer who's on death row
"_____

_____"

Yourself
"_____

_____."

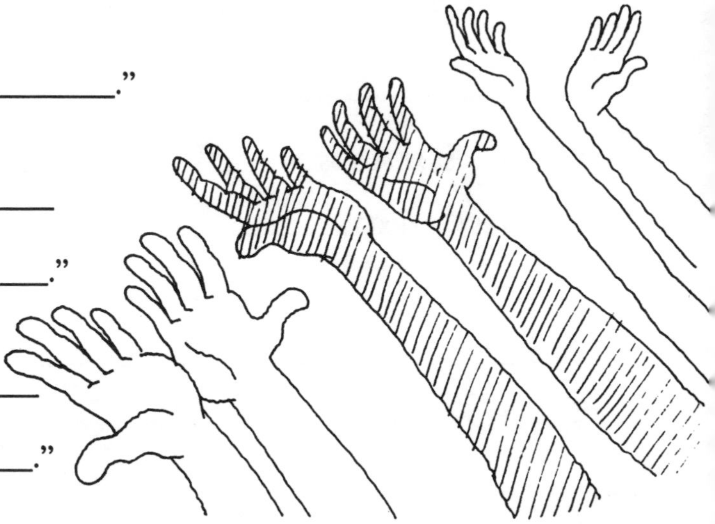

REVELATION 9

Trumpets and Terror

The fifth and sixth trumpets are sounded (following the first four in the previous chapter), resulting first in the release of "locusts" with the power to torment people who do not have the seal of God. Later a third of all people die at the hands of a vast army numbering two hundred million. Yet the ones who live through this terror still do not repent and turn to God.

Form small groups. Hand a skit description (cut from a copy of the reproducible sheet, "Time Tunnel") to each small group. In each case, a person from the past travels to our time—and back, where he or she tries to explain what he or she has seen. As the skits are acted out, be sure that all descriptions are confined to the knowledge and experience of that time. Use this activity to show how John must have felt as he tried to describe dramatic events of the future with his first-century vocabulary.

DATE I USED THIS SESSION _____ GROUP I USED IT WITH _____

NOTES FOR NEXT TIME _____

_____

_____

1. What's the scariest place you've ever been? What made it so frightening? (Examples: a cemetery; the edge of a cliff; the top of a tall building, etc.)

2. Revelation 9 tells of a truly frightening place—the "Abyss" (vs. 1). Who do you think controls the Abyss? (Nothing is outside God's control. The key has to be given to the "star," whom many interpret to be Satan, who is "hurled to the earth" [12:9]. [According to verse 11, the name of the "angel of the Abyss" is *Abaddon*, or *Apollyon*, both of which mean "Destroyer."])

3. Why else might you think God is in control, based on what happens when the Abyss is opened (vss. 2-6)? (The power of the "locusts" is limited. They are not allowed to harm the people who carry God's seal.)

4. Is there anything you think of as "a fate worse than death"? (Remind kids that God will see His people through any trial, no matter how bad it seems. The people in verse 6 are not God's people, and they long to die rather than experience the pain being inflicted on them.)

5. Do you think the creatures in verses 3-11 are literally locusts, or do you think the term stands for something else? Explain. (If literal, they are unlike any insects known to us. Some feel these are demons, based on their home in the Abyss [Luke 8:31], their attack of people rather than plants [vs. 4], their unusual description [vss. 7-10], and the fact that they are united under a "king" [vs. 11]. Others suggest the locusts might stand for soldiers.)

6. At the sound of the sixth trumpet, more destruction takes place (vss. 13-16). Do you think these are God's angels, or demons? Why? (God's angels are not "bound.") How can we be sure God is still in control? (These angels are restricted to prevent the premature destruction of people. The time for their release is determined to the very year, month, day, and hour.)

7. Look at verses 16-19. Do you think the number of troops is literal—exactly two hundred million—or simply an army too large to be counted? Are the horses and riders demonic, or was John trying to describe some kind of modern weaponry from his first-century perspective? (Kids may have differing opinions. So do trained Bible scholars. In interpreting details, don't miss the clear facts: another third of humankind will die, after already losing a quarter of the population to the fourth seal [6:7, 8].)

8. **Wouldn't you think that by now God would have the attention of these people? How do they respond** (vss. 20, 21)? (Their sinful lives go on pretty much as usual—with worship of idols and demons, fooling around with magic, murder, sexual immorality, and stealing.)

9. **Do Bible passages like this frighten you? Why?** (Encourage honest comments. These events are frightening to anyone. But remind kids that even during this terrible time, God watches over those who have His mark. Believers shouldn't worry about being separated from Him—no matter how bad our circumstances. [See Romans 8:38, 39.])

Ask: **What would you do if you wanted to "make" somebody fall in love with you?** (Let kids suggest strategies.) **Could it really work? Can you force someone to love you?** Explain that though God loves each of us, He will never force us to love Him. We must choose to. If we resist loving God, we risk the hardheartedness of the people described in this chapter. Have someone read I Corinthians 13:4-7 to review what *real* love is. Then challenge everyone to develop this kind of love—first toward God, and then toward each other.

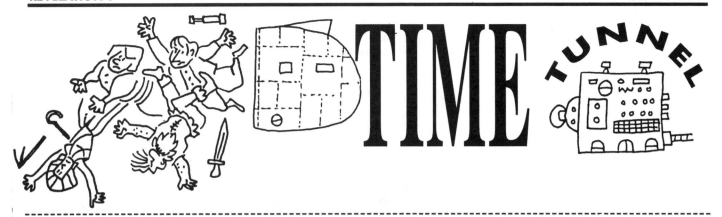

SKIT 1

One of you is Attila the Hun, a warlord from about 1,500 years ago. Attila accidentally stepped into a "time tunnel" and traveled to the present, where he saw a high school football game. Now he has returned to the past, where he must tell his fellow Huns of the "warfare" he has seen. Keep in mind that none of you knows words like "football" or "goalpost."

SKIT 2

One of you is Christopher Columbus, who landed more or less in North America about 500 years ago. Columbus accidentally stepped into a "time tunnel" and traveled to the present, where he sailed on an ocean liner called *The Love Boat*. Now he has returned to the past, where he must tell his crew members of the "floating city" he has seen. Keep in mind that none of you knows words like "luxury liner" or "swimming pool."

SKIT 3

One of you is a chambermaid from the Middle Ages, about 1,000 years ago. This young woman accidentally stepped into a "time tunnel" and traveled to the present, where she flew on a jumbo 747 jet. Now she has returned to the past, where she must tell her fellow castle dwellers of the "armored bird" she has seen. Keep in mind that none of you knows words like "plane" or "flight attendant."

SKIT 4

One of you is Cleopatra, queen of Egypt over 2,000 years ago. Cleopatra accidentally stepped into a "time tunnel" and traveled to the present, where she watched a rerun of *Beverly Hills 90210* on TV. Now she has returned to the past, where she must tell her fellow Egyptians of the "little people" she has seen on "the magic box." Keep in mind that none of you knows words like "television" or "electricity."

REVELATION 10

A Sweet and Sour Scroll

After witnessing the heavenly activity that takes place between the judgments of the sixth and seventh trumpets, John isn't allowed to reveal everything he hears. Yet he does describe a mighty angel who gives him a scroll and commands him to eat it, after which John is told to prophesy again about what he sees.

(Needed: Team prize [optional])

Form teams. Give each team one of the four sets of "story makings" cut from a copy of the reproducible sheet, "Tall Tales." Teams must put their information face down until you say "Go." Explain that each team will have to write a "tall tale" using the title and ten words provided. You'll allow just two minutes for this. Give the "Go" signal. After two minutes, have teams share their tall tales; check to see that all words were used. If you like, give a prize for the best story that uses all the words. Explain that the Book of Revelation requires us to deal with descriptions that may seem even "taller" than some of our fiction—but Revelation is true. The scenes witnessed and related by John in this chapter are an example.

DATE I USED THIS SESSION _____ GROUP I USED IT WITH _____

NOTES FOR NEXT TIME _____

_____

_____

1. Who's the most physically impressive person you've ever seen? Explain.

2. John had already witnessed a number of creatures who were sure to get noticed—assorted creatures who had six wings and were covered with eyes (4:7, 8), a Lamb with seven horns and seven eyes (5:6), etc. What unusual being does he encounter and describe in verses 1-3? (A "mighty angel" who, by all indications, is immense.)

3. Do you think this angel was a "good guy" or a "bad guy"? Why? (The rainbow and the direction from which he had come ["down from heaven"] suggest that this is one of God's angels. His later actions will confirm it. [Some suggest this is an appearance of Jesus Himself, though others don't agree.])

4. This angel sounded impressive, too (vss. 3, 4). Yet when John started to record what the seven thunders said, he was told not to. What do you think was the reason? Does it bother you that some information is being withheld from you? (There's a proper time for everything, and apparently the time for this information is not yet here. Besides, the Book of Revelation contains so much information already that few people agree on what it all means.)

5. What was the angel's message that *is* revealed to us (vss. 5-7)? (There will be "no more delay." With the sounding of the seventh trumpet, everything that God has promised about His kingdom ["the mystery of God"] will be accomplished.) Are you looking forward to this event or not? Why?

6. What instructions did John receive regarding the angel he saw (vs. 8, 9)? (The angel was carrying a little scroll [vs. 2] which John was told to take and eat. The scroll would taste sweet, yet it would turn John's stomach sour.) Have you ever felt God wanted you to do something that you didn't completely understand? When? Do you ever wish you could understand everything God might want of you before agreeing to any of it? Explain.

7. What do you think the "tastes sweet, turns sour" phenomenon (vs. 10) is supposed to represent? ("Eating" God's Word was not a new concept for those who knew the Old Testament. [See Jeremiah 15:15 and Psalm 119:103.] While the Word of God is "sweet," our obedience to it will occasionally involve suffering or pain on our part.)

8. How do you think John might have felt about his assignment to "prophesy again" (vs. 11)? (Though seeing this vision, John was still on the island of Patmos, exiled from friends and coworkers. He was probably excited about the thought of passing on this priceless information about the future.)

9. When you think of serving God, are there parts that *you* can get excited about? Or do you see the whole thing as a chore? Explain.

Say: **You might never get a command to eat your Bible, though John was told to eat a scroll in Revelation 10:9. But you probably have to admit that some of the commands you're given in the Bible are a little "tastier" than others. Think of everything you can recall that Christians are instructed to do. Which are "sweet" things (the ones you enjoy)? Which are "sour" to you (things you dislike, maybe even dread)?** Let kids list these in two columns on sheets of paper. When they finish, have some of them read their lists. Then discuss: **Do you try to get away with obeying only "easy" commands? How could we help each other "develop a taste for" some of these commands?**

TALL TALES

TALL TALE TITLE: **PAUL BUNYAN GOES TO TOWN.** WORDS YOU MUST INCLUDE:

> KITCHEN
> HARPOON
> PANCAKES
> WRESTLING
> MOUSSE
> ORANGE
> GUITAR
> PIG
> SOFA
> CAMERA

TALL TALE TITLE: **THE WOLFMAN'S REVENGE.** WORDS YOU MUST INCLUDE:

> COLA
> MONOPOLY
> AMNESIA
> FINGERNAILS
> SOCKS
> CHEESE
> SPIDER-MAN
> TENNIS
> THURSDAY
> PHOTOCOPIER

TALL TALE TITLE: **ROBIN HOOD GOES ON A DATE.** WORDS YOU MUST INCLUDE:

> BOW
> SPAGHETTI
> ELF
> TURTLE
> SPACESHIP
> VOLLEYBALL
> ARREST
> BRAIN
> TELEPHONE
> LIGHTNING

TALL TALE TITLE: **JOHNNY APPLESEED MEETS FRANKENSTEIN.** WORDS YOU MUST INCLUDE:

> NASTY
> FISH
> BUBBLE
> HIKE
> SCAR
> PIZZA
> VENTRILOQUIST
> FONDUE
> TAXI
> TEACHER

REVELATION 11

You and Me Against the World

John is assigned to measure the temple and altar, and to count the worshipers. He is informed of God's "two witnesses" who will make a bold and powerful stand for Him during forty-two months when unbelievers are hostile toward the things of God. After being put to death and left in the streets for 3 1/2 days, they are miraculously resurrected and taken into heaven. Afterward, the seventh trumpet sounds and another series of signs begins.

(Needed: Prizes [optional])

Have a "Safest Prediction" contest. See who can come up with the best no-risk prediction for the coming year. (Examples: "There will be a TV show about two detectives, one street-wise and one who goes by the book"; "Someone will claim to have seen Elvis in a doughnut shop"; "A certain Great Lakes state will have a large snowfall sometime during the winter.") Award prizes if you like. Then discuss how general some "prophecies" (horoscopes, tabloids, fortune cookies) tend to get to ensure at least some degree of success. Contrast these "wild guesses" with the very specific events and time periods given in this chapter of Revelation.

DATE I USED THIS SESSION _____ GROUP I USED IT WITH _____

NOTES FOR NEXT TIME _____

_____

_____

Q&A

1. When was the last time you had a minority opinion—a view that was different from almost everyone else's in the room? How do you feel when it seems that no one else agrees with you? Do you ever find it hard to believe that you might be right while everyone else is wrong?

2. John is assigned to "take inventory" of God's possessions (the temple) and His people (the worshipers). From a Jewish viewpoint, what would you think about the scene John describes (vss. 1, 2)? (The idea that the temple and city had been given to the Gentiles would be very upsetting. On the other hand, no Jewish temple currently exists in Jerusalem, the "holy city." Those who hold that Revelation takes place in the future and expect literal fulfillment assume that the temple will be rebuilt. Other interpreters treat this symbolically.)

3. God sends two "witnesses" to speak for Him. How do they differ from two kids your youth group might send door-to-door to invite others to attend (vss. 3-6)? (For one thing, these witnesses will display God's power in incredible ways—shooting fire from their mouths and doing miracles like those performed by Moses and Elijah.)

4. How would you feel if you stood up against a bully or a group of people and convinced them to back down? What would other people think of you? How would you feel if you tried the same thing, but didn't succeed? Why?

5. For a while, God will protect the two witnesses from the hostile people they encounter. But then what happens (vss. 7-10)? (Not only are they killed, but their bodies are left in the streets and people throw parties to celebrate. [This is the first mention of the "beast," who is more fully described in chapters 13 and 17.])

6. People who oppose God never have the "last laugh." Suppose you were at a "The Witnesses Are Dead" party, watching their bodies via satellite on large-screen television. How would you respond to the events described in verses 11-14? Why? (Most people will respond in terror at the combination of resurrection, ascension, and earthquake. They'll realize that God is responsible.)

7. Nothing is said here about large numbers of people forsaking their evil ways and becoming Christians. Do you think the hard work and humiliating deaths of the two witnesses were for nothing? Explain. (If nothing else, God was glorified by them. And if a small number of people—even one—believed in Jesus and received eternal life, wouldn't the sacrifice be worthwhile? [While we may see the truth of this in regard to other "witnesses," do we see it for ourselves as well?])

8. John's account shifts from earth back to heaven, where the seventh angel sounds the trumpet for the last in this series of judgments. Based on the comments of the heavenly creatures, what do you think will happen in coming chapters (vss. 15-19)? (They seem to say that the time has come for full power to be restored to God over the "kingdom of the world.")

Some say this chapter of Revelation is among the hardest to interpret. Some interpretations are very literal; others depend on varying levels of symbolism. If you wish, discuss your own interpretations of the 3 1/2 years (42 months, 1,260 days, etc.), the identity of the witnesses, the desecration of the temple, etc. The reproducible sheet, "Witness Protection Program," seeks to apply the experience of the two witnesses. After kids fill it out, discuss. Then encourage them to actually ask their "partner prospects" to help them with the task of being witnesses.

WITNESS PROTECTION PROGRAM

Sure, those two witnesses from Revelation 11 had it easy. Not like we have it today. No wonder so few of us want to stick our necks out and share our faith with those who don't know Jesus. It's tough to risk stumbling over our words. To hear people laugh. To be labeled "weird" and kept out of the cool groups at school.

Keeping in mind the story of those two witnesses, check all of the following answers that apply. Fill in one of your own, too.

I would share my faith more if:

❑ I had a partner.
❑ I could destroy the Lord's enemies by shooting fire out of my mouth.
❑ I could keep it from raining, and turn rivers into blood.
❑ I could strike the earth with every kind of plague whenever I wanted.
❑ I could count on being killed.
❑ I knew that my dead body would lie in the street for 3 1/2 days.
❑ I knew that my death would cause people to party.
❑ I could count on being resurrected.
❑ I could hear a voice from heaven.
❑ I could go to heaven while everybody watched.
❑ Other _____.

Now, let's narrow it down to one way in which you could pretty easily follow the example of the two witnesses: having a partner.

If I had a partner, the two of us could:

❑ Pray for each other as we try to tell people about Jesus.
❑ Pray that we'll have opportunities to talk about what we believe.
❑ Ask each other questions that people might ask about God, then find answers.
❑ Practice telling each other what Jesus has done in our lives.
❑ Encourage each other when our witnessing doesn't seem to go very well.
❑ Celebrate when it does.
❑ Actually go with each other when we try to share our faith.
❑ Other _____.

Now, let's really narrow it down. Who could you ask to be such a partner to you?

_____

_____

My top three partner prospects are:

_____

_____

_____

REVELATION 12

This Means War

The ongoing conflict between Satan and God is described with vivid imagery in this chapter. After Satan is unable to defeat God's heavenly forces, he tries to destroy God's people. During the last days, such persecution will become particularly intense.

(Needed: Small object)

Form two equal teams; have each team "number off" (so that each person has a number). Teams should line up at opposite ends of the room. In the center should be a small object—a beanbag, cloth napkin, etc. Explain that you will call out a number (two, for instance). At that point the "number two" person on each team runs out to the object. The goal is to pick up the object and get back to one's own team without being tagged by the other person. A successful return is worth two points for the team that obtained the object; a tag is worth one point for the team of the person who does the tagging. As soon as one person touches the center object, he or she becomes vulnerable to being tagged by the other person. Occasionally call more than one number to see what happens. This activity should demonstrate the urgency that goes into one-on-one conflicts—as you prepare to discuss the biggest conflict of all.

DATE I USED THIS SESSION _____ GROUP I USED IT WITH _____

NOTES FOR NEXT TIME _____

_____

_____

1. Do you ever feel as if you're part of something really big? If so, when?

2. Sometimes we can convince ourselves that we don't matter much. But when we resist the devil, we're part of something *really* big. Told from God's perspective, the struggle sounds pretty exciting. As you read through verses 1-6, what do you think the following symbols represent:

• **The pregnant woman?** (Most say Israel; some say the church; some say Mary.)
• **The enormous, red dragon?** (Satan.)
• **The male child?** (Jesus.)

3. If God's power is greater than Satan's, why do we care what the devil does? (While God's *ultimate* victory is assured, the struggles His people face in the meantime are intense. This is shown by the extent of the dragon's power in verse 4.)

4. Chapter 11 warned of intense persecution that would last for 3 1/2 years (1,260 days). The same number of days pops up in this chapter as well (vs. 6), but why? (Though this is a period of persecution for God's people, it's also a time of God's protection.)

5. Wasn't Satan defeated when Jesus died on the cross? (See John 16:11.) If so, why is he still pestering us, and why will he be so powerful during the great tribulation? (It's as if he's been found guilty, yet is awaiting sentencing. By the end of Revelation, the verdict will have been executed. Until then, he lives to make trouble for God's people.)

6. What is one of Satan's first steps toward his final downfall that will take place during this time (vss. 7-9)? (After going to battle against Michael and the heavenly angels, Satan and his followers are hurled down to earth.)

7. How does the idea of "war in heaven" strike you? Does it mean that God isn't strong enough to prevent an invasion? (If there's an invasion, it's only because God allows it.

Note that Satan and his angels can't even overcome God's angels, much less God Himself.)

8. **Knowing that his time is short, Satan becomes even more aggressive** (vss. 10-12). **Who is the object of his anger** (vss. 13-17)**? Why?** (He tries to attack "the woman who had given birth" to Jesus. Everyone who remains loyal to God becomes a target.)

9. **The figurative language here makes it difficult to understand exactly what will happen. But what is one fact that remains clear?** (God will never allow His people to be completely eliminated—even during this time when satanic power is at its height.)

10. **Verses 10-12 sound almost like a song of praise. If you were going to write such a song, what would you mention that God has done for you?**

(Needed: Markers)

Give kids markers and the reproducible sheet, "The Accuser." Let kids work on this individually. They may or may not want to share how they've felt accused in these areas. Point out that these accusations can come from people, too, and should also be rejected because the "blood of the Lamb" blots out the sins of those who belong to Him [Christ]. Also note that "Maybe you don't belong to Jesus after all" is a charge that we *should* consider if we haven't put our faith in Christ. Ask: **How could your life change if you really felt 100% loved and forgiven by God?**

THE ACCUSER

Until the forces of heaven pin him to the mat for good, the devil will keep accusing us of all kinds of things. Some of his charges will make sense on the surface; others will be total baloney. One of his goals will be to keep us off balance, feeling guilty and unworthy— pinning *us* to the mat.

Do you see on this wall any of his accusations against you?

Now read Revelation 12:10-12. A crushing defeat is in store for your accuser. Based on these verses, use a marker to "paint out" the accusations on this wall that aren't worth worrying about.

REVELATION 13

Telltale Marks

The dragon (Satan) recruits an assistant—a "beast." Then a second beast arrives on the scene—a deceptive figure who directs people's attention to the first beast. The power and miraculous signs of these three convince almost everyone to worship them. And people are forced to receive a kind of loyalty mark on their right hands or foreheads in order to buy or sell.

Play "picture charades" (like the popular game, Pictionary) with a twist. Assign individuals, one at a time, to draw creatures that are a *cross* between one animal and another. The rest of the group must try to guess what two animals are being combined. Examples: A dog and a cow; a fish and a bird; a turtle and an earthworm; a cat and a clam; a horse and a pig. No letters or numbers may be used while drawing. Then explain that this session pertains to a different kind of "beast" that resembles a combination of several animals.

DATE I USED THIS SESSION _____ GROUP I USED IT WITH _____

NOTES FOR NEXT TIME _____

_____

_____

1. Have you or any of your friends ever been attracted to someone who was likely to get you in trouble in some way? If so, why? (Many young people have friends that draw attention to themselves by drinking, smoking, or other forms of rebellion. Some kids, when dating, are drawn to rebel personalities with reputations for being "experienced.")

2. Attraction to dangerous personalities will increase during the period described in Revelation 13. Satan will use someone to act as his spokesperson—someone identified by John as a "beast." Some scholars see the beast as a symbol of the Roman Empire, which called its secular authorities gods. Others see the beast as the antichrist. How are people going to respond to this beast (vss. 1-4)? Why? (Because of his great power, and perhaps because it seems he has miraculously recovered from what should have been a fatal wound, they give him unquestioned devotion. [The animal references—leopard, bear, and lion—may represent the previous ungodly empires of Greece, Medo-Persia, and Babylon as in Daniel 7:4-6.])

3. Will this beast try to deceive people by seeming to be "godly" (vss. 5-10)? Explain. (During this time, believing in God is not at all a "plus" in the political arena. In spite of his "proud words and blasphemies," all but a very few people worship the beast.)

4. So we have the dragon (Satan) and the beast, but then another beast appears (later referred to as the false prophet). (See 19:20 and 20:10.) While the first beast has a political following, the second seems to back the first from a religious perspective. What "special effects" does the second beast use (vss. 11-15)? (With even greater miraculous signs, and by setting up the first beast's image [which appears to talk] as an object of worship for the people.)

5. Yet worship of the first beast is not just a matter of choice. What other methods of "persuasion" does the second beast use to convince people to be loyal to the first (vss. 16-18)? (People are not allowed to buy or sell without having the mark of the beast [his name or the number 666] on their right hands or foreheads.)

6. At this point, how do you think people who are loyal to God will be affected? (Those without the mark of the beast will become much easier to identify. Without a means of buying or selling, they are certain to face even more difficult times.)

7. With all the advanced computer programs we can run these days, how hard do you think people should try to figure out how the number 666 translates into any names currently in existence? (Depending on what number values are assigned to alphabetic letters, it is possible to make many names "number" 666. When attempting to identify the beast, it's unwise to jump to any unsubstantiated conclusions. The number has been interpreted in many ways, including as literal names like "Nero Caesar," and as a symbol of imperfection and evil—since 6 is just short of the "number of perfection," 7.)

8. Do you think anyone who is still trying to stand for the real God should give up at this point? If someone is looking to go to heaven anyway, why put up with all the terrible persecution? What hope would godly people have? (As bleak as the situation seems in chapter 13, the next chapter shows quite a contrast. If people can remain faithful during such a terrible time, so should we remain faithful wherever God has placed us.)

The reproducible sheet, "Watch for the Mark," asks kids to think about "marks" that might warn them that some activities are harmful. Let them share and explain their answers (answers may vary). Ask: **What other "marks" do people bear as a result of doing wrong? How could these "marks" help warn you to stay away from such activities?**

When you read through Revelation, you see how tremendously evil the antichrist is going to be. Multitudes of people will actually worship him and wear his "mark." But what about now? By what "marks" can you identify something wrong that others might think is harmless?

Can you match the activities listed below with "marks" that often go with them? Draw lines from the activities to the pictures of the "marks" you'd match them with. Feel free to use the same "marks" more than once.

ACTIVITIES:	MARKS:

Getting drunk

Loving money

Belonging to a cult

Using illegal drugs

Having sex before marriage

Not controlling your temper

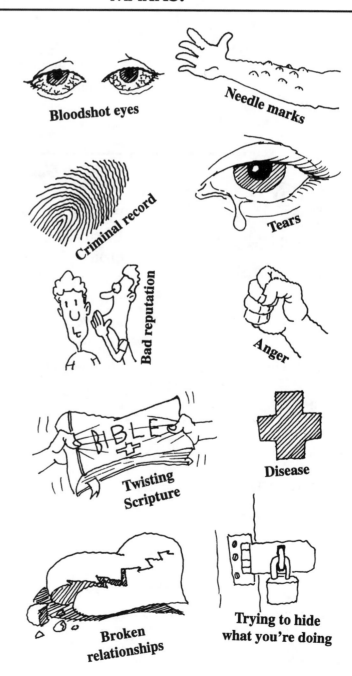

Bloodshot eyes

Needle marks

Criminal record

Tears

Bad reputation

Anger

Twisting Scripture

Disease

Broken relationships

Trying to hide what you're doing

REVELATION 14

Hammered By a Sickle

This chapter makes it clear where the real power lies. God is still in control, and the people with His seal remain completely safe. It also becomes obvious that the reign of the "beast" will be short, because God's judgment is at hand. The destruction of the wicked will be like swinging a sickle through a field and watching the plants topple to the ground.

(Needed: Guitar or other accompaniment; prizes [optional])

Pass out copies of "Tailor-Made Tunes," the reproducible sheet. Have each person fill in his or her own words in the blanks. Then try singing the songs together—with each person singing his or her own words. After this noisy effort, ask a few individuals to share their lyrics. Award a prize for the best new version of each song if you wish. Explain that having an exclusive song will be one of the privileges of God's faithful "remnant" during the time described in this chapter.

DATE I USED THIS SESSION _____ GROUP I USED IT WITH _____

NOTES FOR NEXT TIME _____

_____

_____

1. What's the largest musical event you've ever participated in—as either a musician or a spectator?

2. In Revelation 7, God placed His seal on 144,000 people. As chapter 14 opens, what would you say is the mood of these "sealed" people (vss. 1-5)? (They were more than just "surviving." They were pure, joyful, and singing.)

3. What mood are you usually in when you sing songs in church? Why? Does your mood usually go with the words you're singing? How do you feel about that?

4. One key to the mood of these people was the fact that "they follow the Lamb wherever He goes" (vs. 4). If you followed Jesus more closely, how do you think *your* levels of joy, peace, and confidence would be affected?

5. John's focus shifts from the 144,000 people to three angels. So many of the angels previously described in Revelation (the ones with the seals and the trumpets, for example) had terrible news to tell. Did *these* three have good news or bad news (vss. 6-13)? Explain. (It would depend on the person's relationship with God. It was time for God's judgment, the fall of "Babylon" [interpreted variously as the city of Rome, the city of Babylon, or the false religious system], and retribution for all who had followed the beast. This will be good news, however, for God's people.)

6. Those who followed the beast freely worshiped him, as well as Satan (13:4), blasphemed against the true God (13:6), and showed extreme hostility toward those who believed in God (12:17). What will be the consequences (vss. 9-11)? (This passage teaches that the consequence of rejecting God to follow Satan's spokesperson is everlasting torment.)

7. What kinds of excuses do you think people will make for rejecting God and following Satan? (It didn't seem like such a big deal; everybody was doing it; I was threatened with punishment, etc.) When do kids use excuses like these today?

8. It's a terrible thing to ponder the intensity of what's in store for those who willingly reject God. So what are our options (vs. 13)? (Those who "die in the Lord" have nothing to fear. Rather, they will be "blessed." And salvation is available to everyone as a free gift of God, so we are without excuse.)

9. Do you think God will have a tough time overcoming the opposition that has been raised by Satan and his associates (vss. 14-20)? Why? (When the time is right, the wicked people of the world will be felled as easily as a stalk of wheat falls at the blade of a sickle. [Note the huge numbers of such people suggested by the image of blood as high as a horse's bridle for a distance of 180 miles.])

10. When you think about this judgment, how do you feel? (a) It serves them right; (b) how tragic it will be for them; (c) at least *I* won't be included; (d) I should get busy and tell others about Jesus while there's still time; (e) other (explain).

Say: **The story is told of a guy named Damocles [DAM-uh-cleez] who was always mouthing off about how great it must be to be king. The king at the time, Dionysius [die-uh-NISH-ee-us], heard of this, and invited Damocles to be "king for a day." A banquet was held, with Damocles at the head of the table. In the midst of all this, Damocles happened to look up. Directly above him hung a large sword, suspended by a single hair. Damocles stopped enjoying the "benefits" of being king pretty quickly. The moral: For anyone, especially those in high positions, disaster can strike anytime.**

Rather than the sword of Damocles, the "sickle" of God will someday sweep down on people who have rejected Him. If your faith is in Christ, you'll escape destruction. But what about everyone else? Now that you know about the sickle of God, what changes might you need to make in the way you relate to people who don't know Christ?

Tailor-Made Tunes

TWINKLE, TWINKLE, LITTLE _____

Twinkle, twinkle, little _____,
How I wonder what you _____.
Up above the _____ so _____,
Like a _____ in the _____,
Twinkle, twinkle, little _____,
How I wonder what you _____.

YANKEE DOODLE

Yankee Doodle went to _____
Riding on a _____,
Stuck a _____ in his _____
And called it _____.

HOME ON THE _____

Oh, give me a _____
Where the _____ roam,
Where the _____ and the _____ play;
Where seldom is _____
A discouraging _____
And the _____ is not _____ all day.

Home, home on the _____,
Where the _____ and the _____ play;
Where seldom is _____
A discouraging _____
And the _____ is not _____ all day.

Winning Through Losing

So far in the Book of Revelation there have been seven churches, seven seals, seven trumpets, and a few more "sevens." This chapter introduces a final set of "seven": angels who will administer the seven "bowls filled with the wrath of God." Though this is a period of history that will experience the most intense reign of evil ever seen, God is preparing to put an end to "Babylon" and remind everyone that He is in control.

(Needed: Team prize [optional])

Have a "Seven Scavenger Hunt." Challenge teams to see who can bring the most items in groups of seven back to your meeting place within a time limit you've set. (Examples: seven bottle caps, seven hymnbooks, seven shoes, seven rocks, seven signatures from neighbors, etc.) Award a prize to the winning team if you like (a can of Seven-Up for each person might be appropriate). Then lead into the discussion of seven angels and seven plagues.

DATE I USED THIS SESSION _____ GROUP I USED IT WITH _____

NOTES FOR NEXT TIME _____

_____

_____

1. When was the last time you were an object of someone's "wrath"? What effect did it have on you?

2. Chapters 15 and 16 of Revelation deal mainly with God's wrath directed toward those who worship Satan and the "beast" during the last days. This will include "seven last plagues" (vs. 1). What do you think of when you hear the word *plague*? (Locusts; diseases such as the bubonic plague, or perhaps AIDS; the Old Testament plagues on Egypt, etc.)

3. John saw seven angels, the seven plagues, a "sea of glass," and a bunch of people "who had been victorious over the beast and his image" (vss. 1, 2). How had this group of people managed to be victorious over such a powerful figure? (They had died. We don't often associate dying with winning, but the fact that these people had resisted giving in to the beast—even at penalty of death—was a victory for them.)

4. Have you ever wondered what it would be like to face death for your faith? What do you think it might be like? What do you think you would do?

5. Do you think these people had any regrets that their earthly lives had been so threatening and miserable? Why? (See verses 2-4. They were overjoyed to at last be in the presence of God, and they sang praises to Him. Though in a tiny minority, they had recognized that God's ways were "just and true," and they had not given up their faith in Him.)

6. Do you ever have any regrets that your life isn't better than it is? Explain. (Many young people want to live elsewhere, to have more money, to be rid of certain people, etc. Some deal with the feelings quickly and move on, though others "get stuck" with such thoughts for a longer period. They all need to realize that better things await them.)

7. The image we have of executioners is grim: hooded heads, and so forth. Is this true of the angels that will administer God's final bowls of wrath (vss. 5-8)? Explain. (No. God's judgments are righteous. There is no chance in this case of a mistake. The angels wear brilliant white and gold, because their actions in no way affect their purity.)

8. **In what ways do you think God shows His wrath today? Do you think you've ever felt the wrath of God? If so, how?** (Make it clear that while God will certainly discipline the people He loves [Hebrews 12:4-11], we have been saved from His wrath [Romans 5:9]. Also discuss differences between natural disasters [floods, tornados, etc.] and divine judgment as displayed during this period of Revelation.)

Those who beat the beast by refusing to cave in to him celebrate their victory in this chapter. But their victory didn't come easily. We may want spiritual victory, too, but we often want it to come easily. The reproducible sheet, "The Thrill of Victory," shows how the intensity of the struggle determines the thrill of the victory. When kids finish the sheet, make some spiritual parallels. If you know of missionaries or others in your church who have faced great spiritual trials and have seen, to some degree, positive results because of their sacrifices, try to mention them. Ask kids: **If you put the same effort into resisting temptation that you do into your favorite sport or hobby, what would change? Have you ever felt a "thrill of victory" over something you did for God? What was it like?**

THE THRILL OF VICTORY

We all like to be winners. Yet "the thrill of victory" isn't always what we'd like it to be. Unless we have to struggle a little and have some decent competition, a "victory" may not seem like much. Consider each of the following victories, and rate how excited you would get about each one using a scale of 1 (yawns and snores) to 10 (adrenalin shooting through your body like water through a fire hose).

1 2 3 4 5 6 7 8 9 10   Your little brother challenges you to some one-on-one basketball, and you beat him 20 to 0.

1 2 3 4 5 6 7 8 9 10   Michael Jordan challenges you to a game, and you score two points against him.

1 2 3 4 5 6 7 8 9 10   After four years of lessons, hard work, and practice, you bowl a 300 game.

1 2 3 4 5 6 7 8 9 10   The first time you try water skiing, you "get up" on your third try.

1 2 3 4 5 6 7 8 9 10   You play on a team against your school's biggest rival, and blow them away by the largest margin ever. The outcome is never in doubt.

1 2 3 4 5 6 7 8 9 10   You play your school's biggest rival and get way behind, but catch up and win in the final three seconds.

1 2 3 4 5 6 7 8 9 10   You go mountain climbing, find a path where someone has already gone up, and reach the top with no trouble.

1 2 3 4 5 6 7 8 9 10   You go mountain climbing, carve a path where no one has ever been before, and reach the top exhausted.

1 2 3 4 5 6 7 8 9 10   You're playing a tough sport against a team you've never beaten. It's close all the way, but you finally win. Then you overhear one of them say to another that they had let you win.

REVELATION 16

The Super Bowls

The seven angels introduced in the previous chapter administer "the seven bowls of God's wrath." The plagues that result: horrible sores on the followers of the beast, pollution of all water sources, intense heat, darkness, warfare, the worst earthquake ever, and 100-pound hailstones. Yet people still curse God rather then repenting and turning to Him.

(Needed: Bowls, buckets, towels, and a team prize)

(Note: This contest works best outside. If you have to be inside, substitute styrofoam "peanuts" or birdseed for the water.) Form relay teams. Give each team a plastic bowl (bowls should be the same size). At one end of the relay course, place a water source (a faucet or bucket of water). At the other end, place a bucket for each team (buckets should be the same size). At your signal, the first person on each team should put water in the bowl, place the bowl on his or her head, walk it to the other end of the course, and drop the water in the empty bucket. Then he or she returns the bowl for the next person to do the same, and on down the line. After a few minutes, measure the water in each bucket, and award a prize to the team that's accumulated the most. Explain that this session deals with seven bowls that contain something a lot worse than water.

DATE I USED THIS SESSION _____ GROUP I USED IT WITH _____

NOTES FOR NEXT TIME_____

_____

_____

1. What do you think are the worst things that are happening to our environment? (Examples: Oil spills, destruction of rain forests, etc.) **Why do you think some people fight so hard against these problems?** (A possibility: If we want the earth to last, we need to take care of it.)

2. What do you think Christians should do about the environment? (The world is God's creation; people are stewards of it. We shouldn't abuse or waste what He has provided. Yet the earth isn't intended to last forever; we should also be concerned for the salvation of the people of the earth.)

3. During the period described in this chapter, sinful people and the earth itself are going to feel the effects of God's wrath. The first "bowl of wrath" strikes the people. If you had to have a terribly painful sore somewhere on your body where it doesn't show, or a mild (but really ugly) rash all over your face and hands, which would you select? Why? (Compare to verses 1 and 2, where the followers of the beast receive sores that are ugly *and* painful.)

4. Do you think these people spent a lot of time bathing their sores (vss. 3-7)? Why? (All the water sources "became blood.")

5. In an area without drinkable water, what's the last thing you would want to cope with (vss. 8, 9)? (Probably "intense heat.") **By this time, people have a pretty good idea that the real God is behind these events. How do they respond?** (These people are so opposed to God that they have no intention of repenting.)

6. The sixth bowl prepares the way for the final war to be fought on earth—Armageddon (vss. 12-16). **How is the war promoted?** (Demons will be at work to involve the kings of the earth and gather them for battle.)

7. The seventh bowl sets some records. What are they (vss. 17-21)? (Among other things, 100-pound hailstones and the most severe earthquake ever seen, which will change islands and mountains.)

8. The response: People still "cursed God" (vs. 21). **Are they stupid, or what?** (They aren't interested in submitting to God. Their only interest in God is in wanting Him to leave them alone so that they can do as they please.) **How are people like this today?**

9. **If God shows such wrath against sinful people, what should be** *our* **attitude toward them? Why?** (Let kids struggle with this. While we should reject sin, we need to attract people to Christ instead of condemning them. Only God's judgments are holy and perfect.)

The reproducible sheet, "Bowls of Wrath," will challenge kids to wrestle with their own displays of anger. After giving kids time to choose their responses, discuss. Opinions may vary widely; in some cases *both* choices may be wrong. The point is to provoke kids to think. Ask: **Is showing intense anger toward others ever justified? If so, when? When we are really mad at other people, what options do we have other than "pouring out" our wrath? What are some things God does before He even considers pouring out His wrath** (Warning people, offering forgiveness, being patient, etc.)**? How can we do the same?**

BOWLS OF WRATH

God's anger toward people who refuse to repent is obvious in Revelation 16, where it's "poured out" from seven "bowls." But what about *your* anger? When should you pour it out, and when should you keep it in the bowl? For each of the following actions, circle your response: W for Wrong, R for Right, D for It Depends. Be ready to explain your answers.

W R D   Getting into a shouting match with a parade of racist "skinheads"

W R D   Getting into a fistfight with a parade of racist "skinheads"

W R D   Bombing an abortion clinic when no one is likely to be there

W R D   Carrying a picket sign that says, "Abortion is Murder" in front of an open abortion clinic

W R D   Yelling, "Hey, take your hands off her!" when you see a man slapping a woman in a
             parking lot

W R D   Carrying a gun in case you see things like a man slapping a woman in a parking lot

W R D   Saying, "You think you're so smart, but you're not!" when a non-Christian kid calls
             you a "Holy Roller" in front of other kids

W R D   Saying, "You'll be sorry someday!" when a non-Christian kid calls you a "Holy Roller"
             in front of other kids

W R D   Writing an angry letter to the newspaper about a principal who won't let you have a Bible
             study on the school grounds

W R D   Defying the principal and having your Bible study anyway

W R D   Making an obscene gesture to a kid who just dropped a water balloon on you from a
             window three stories above

W R D   Spray-painting a jagged stripe on the car belonging to the kid who dropped a water balloon
             on you

To think about:

"The Lord . . . [is] slow to anger, abounding in love and faithfulness, maintaining love to thousands, and forgiving wickedness, rebellion and sin. Yet he does not leave the guilty unpunished" (Exodus 34:6, 7).

"Everyone should be quick to listen, slow to speak and slow to become angry, for man's anger does not bring about the righteous life that God desires" (James 1:19, 20).

REVELATION 17

A Bad Connection

In another vision filled with symbols, John is shown the connection between the "great prostitute" and the beast. Though they begin as allies, the beast eventually assumes all power and has no more use for the prostitute. Even their combined efforts against the true God will be used by Him to accomplish His plans as Jesus prepares to return to earth.

Call for a couple of volunteers. Person A asks Person B a question. B should give no response to the first question. Then Person A asks a second question, after which the B answers the *first* question. See how many questions the pair can ask and answer without messing up. Then let other pairs try. Creative question-askers can plan some amusing responses. (For example: "What is the square root of 16?" *No response.* "What would you say is Joe's IQ?" *"Four."* How many guys do you think Beth has dated this week?" *"About 135."*) Later, explain that just as delayed responses can cause confusion, delayed judgment may create false security. Sin may be more deadly than we imagine, as seen in this session.

DATE I USED THIS SESSION _____ GROUP I USED IT WITH _____

NOTES FOR NEXT TIME _____

_____

_____

1. What do you think should be the connection between religion and politics? If you were running for public office, how much would you say about your faith?

2. This chapter of Revelation deals with a bond between a "great prostitute" and "the kings of the earth" (vss. 1, 2). **Who is this prostitute, and what kind of person is she** (vss. 3-6)? **Explain.** (In verse 18 an angel calls her "the great city that rules over the kings of the earth." Some say she stands for an actual city like Jerusalem or Rome or Babylon; others associate her with the corrupt world system in general or with a religious system. She's allied with the "beast" who is covered with blasphemous names; her golden cup is filled with filth; she is "drunk with the blood of the saints.")

3. Why is she labeled "Babylon . . . the mother of prostitutes" (vs. 5)? (Throughout history, many of the world's occultic and false religions originated in Babylon. These religions "seduced" people from the true God.)

4. The attraction of the "woman" might be understandable. But why would anyone be attracted to the beast (vss. 7, 8)? (The fact that "he once was, now is not, and yet will come" makes him a mysterious person. This phrase may refer to his apparently fatal "head wound" from which he recovered [13:3], or it may be an imitation of Jesus, who lived, died, was resurrected, and has promised to return.)

5. Which do you think is usually more attractive: evil or good? Give some examples.

6. The angel speaking to John isn't kidding when he says, "This calls for a mind with wisdom" (vs. 9). Many interpretations are offered for verses 9-14. But what in these verses can you be perfectly sure of? (At some time in the future, groups of powerful people are going to team up against Jesus and lose.)

7. Why do you think the beast and the prostitute, who started out being so close, split up (vss. 15-18)? (If the prostitute represents a religious system, maybe once the beast uses religion to establish his power, he has no further need for it.) **How might we be tempted to "use" Christianity only when we "need" it?**

8. What celebrities can you think of who are treated almost with worship by fans? How can Christians keep from getting overly excited about human leaders and keep their enthusiasm directed toward God instead?

The reproducible sheet, "Making Alliances," will help kids consider how strongly they may be connected to other people in comparison to their attachment to God. When they finish, discuss some of their responses. Ask: **Do you need to strengthen the "bridge" between yourself and God? If so, how can you do that? Might any of your other alliances be a little too strong? Do you think it's possible for a relationship with parents to be too strong? How about a relationship with the church?** Explain that anything that detracts from one's relationship with God needs to be evaluated. Follow with prayer, asking God to provide wisdom to help kids "see through" any attempts of false religion, politics, or anything else that would threaten their relationships with Him.

BAD  CONNECTIONS?

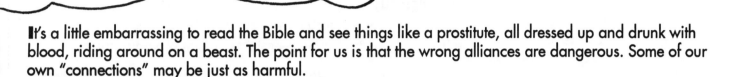

It's a little embarrassing to read the Bible and see things like a prostitute, all dressed up and drunk with blood, riding around on a beast. The point for us is that the wrong alliances are dangerous. Some of our own "connections" may be just as harmful.

In the space below, draw a "bridge" between yourself and each of the other people to show how strong each "alliance" is. Your "bridge" may consist of a single thread, a shaky rope version, a huge stone structure, a four-lane highway, or whatever. It's up to you.

ME   GOD

ME   THE CHURCH

ME   PARENTS

ME   FAVORITE
                                                                RECORDING
                                                                ARTIST

ME   BEST
                                                                CHRISTIAN
                                                                FRIEND

ME   BEST NON-
                                                                CHRISTIAN
                                                                FRIEND

ME   BOYFRIEND OR
                                                                GIRLFRIEND

REVELATION 18

The City That Sank

An angel describes the ultimate fall of "Babylon the Great." God's people are warned to clear out. Later the demise of the city is greatly mourned by the people who had been most closely associated with it—kings, merchants, and sea captains—those who would feel the financial repercussions.

(Needed: Two blindfolds; prize)

Have everyone throw his or her shoes into a pile in the middle of the room. Get two volunteers and blindfold them. These volunteers will compete to see who can find his or her shoes first—using only touch and smell. The rest of the group can cheer the volunteers on, but can't give clues. Before giving the "go" signal, give the pile of shoes a good mixing. Then let the volunteers start their search. After the contest, award a prize to the winner. Ask the competitors how it felt—and smelled—to search through a pile of shoes. Then make the tie-in to this chapter, in which a remnant of God's people are warned to come out of a morally "smelly" city.

DATE I USED THIS SESSION _____ GROUP I USED IT WITH _____

NOTES FOR NEXT TIME _____

_____

_____

1. Have you ever discovered something yucky in the middle of something that outwardly looked OK? (Examples: A bug in some food, mold in bread, rust in a car, etc.) **How did you feel?** (Disgusted, cheated, etc.)

2. Sometimes a whole city can be rotten inside, yet successful on the outside. "Babylon" (which may refer to a literal city, or to an economic or religious system) is described that way. **What are its pros and cons** (vss. 1-3)? (It's described as a luxurious city that has given lots of people a chance to get rich, but it's soon to be destroyed and become an abandoned area.)

3. God's people were called to come out of Babylon (vss. 4-8) so they wouldn't be included in its destruction. **What are some activities or places you or Christian friends are involved in that you might do a lot better to "come out of"?** (Drinking; sexual experimentation; R-rated movies, etc.)

4. Jesus says that those who mourn will be comforted (Matthew 5:4). **What happens to those who claim they will never have to mourn** (Revelation 18:7, 8)? (Being so sure of her invincibility leads Babylon to "death, mourning . . . famine," and God's judgment.)

5. Babylon is personified here. Nearby kings had "committed adultery with her," and they wept and mourned when the city "died" (see vss. 9, 10). **Why were the merchants so upset** (vss. 11-17)? (A rich city was good for business. Without it, they would suffer financially.)

6. How much money would you need to be "financially secure"? **How could wanting to be financially secure keep you from really committing yourself to God?** (You might pass up low-paying or no-pay opportunities to serve God, or spend all your time trying to make money.)

7. Various groups in the chapter comment on the suddenness of the city's fall: "in one hour" (vss. 10, 17, and 19). This may or may not be a literal sixty minutes. But **how could a city fall in just an hour?** (In a bombing raid; in an earthquake; in a nuclear blast; in a tidal wave, etc.)

8. How could your life change radically in an hour or less? If you always kept in mind that your personal "downfall" might be "in one hour," how might your lifestyle change?

9. Look at verses 21-24. Is this message sad or happy? Why? Which of these things (music, work, romance, money, etc.) that are lost would you miss most? Knowing that these things won't last forever, does the time you spend on them need to change? How?

The reproducible sheet, "Evacuate!" helps kids consider the difficulty of leaving a sinful system like that of "Babylon." Discuss kids' responses to the statements. Ask: **How are these comments like the ones you might get from kids at school if you encouraged them to receive Christ as Savior? How are they like the reasons you might give for not walking away from something you're pretty sure is wrong? How much longer do you think you have to "evacuate" habits or friendships that get in the way of your relationship with God?**

Let's say you've been living in the city of Babylon since you were little. Suddenly you get a message from an angel: "Come out of her, my people, so that you will not share in her sins" (Revelation 18:4). In other words, you're supposed to evacuate right away!

But not all of your neighbors agree. How would you answer these comments from your fellow Babylonians?

_____

_____

_____

_____

_____

_____

REVELATION 19

The Cavalry From Calvary

It's time for Jesus to come again. He leads the "armies of heaven" into battle against "the beast and the kings of the earth." The earthly army is defeated and killed. The beast and the false prophet are then judged and thrown into "the fiery lake of burning sulfur."

(Needed: Table)

Copy and cut the cards from the reproducible sheet, "Arms Race." Make at least four sets of cards. Place two sets of cards (each mixed up randomly) face down in a pile on one end of a table. Do the same with the other two sets at the other end of the table. Form two "armies." Each army should line up on one side of the table or the other. One "soldier" from each army approaches that army's pile of cards and draws a card. Both soldiers show their cards simultaneously. Whichever shows the superior weapon (rock beats fist, nuclear missile beats bomber, etc.) wins that round. If identical weapons are drawn, the round is a draw. After giving everyone a chance to draw a card, see which army has won the most "skirmishes." Then point out that this chapter describes a battle in which one army totally outclasses the other.

DATE I USED THIS SESSION _____ GROUP I USED IT WITH _____

NOTES FOR NEXT TIME _____

_____

_____

1. How do you feel when other people compliment you? Why? What if you're praised for things that you don't actually deserve the praise for?

2. Are you a little surprised at some of the things for which God is praised in verses 1-3? Explain. (We may tend to focus on God's love and forgiveness, yet those who witness the plagues and other punishments sent on the wicked are going to praise Him for His "true and just" judgments and vengeance.)

3. Why else do you think the heavenly people are shouting "Hallelujah" (which means "Praise the Lord") (vss. 4-8)? (It's time for "the wedding . . . of the Lamb" which will reward the faithfulness of those who have remained true to Him.) **How does the idea of being "married to the Lamb" hit you? If your relationship with Jesus were a marriage, would it be (a) perfect bliss, (b) no longer exciting, (c) on the rocks, or (d) something else?**

4. John seems to get caught up in the spirit of praise. But he gets a little confused. What can we learn from his mistake (vss. 9, 10)? (Some of the angels John has seen are amazingly wise and powerful, but they aren't divine creatures to be worshiped. They're "fellow servants" with believers.)

5. In Revelation 5 and 6, Jesus has been portrayed as a "Lamb." How does that image compare with the description in 19:11-16? (Other than the robe dipped in blood, which may represent His sacrificial death, there is nothing lamb-like about Him in this account.) **Which of Jesus' titles here means the most to you? Why?**

6. If you were part of the evil, earthly armies and saw Jesus and His armies riding toward you out of heaven, wouldn't you think it was all over for you? What happens instead (vss. 17-19)? (The earthly armies actually try to fight.)

7. The earthly armies are destroyed and fed to the birds. A grim punishment awaits the beast and the false prophet, the "powerful" figures who performed "great and miraculous signs" (13:13) **and who were responsible for misleading so many people. What happens to them (vss. 20, 21)?** (They are thrown alive into the fiery lake of burning sulfur.)

8. **How do you think the martyrs who had been killed by the beast felt at this point? Why?**

9. **When things go wrong for you, do you tend to worry and seek revenge, or to be patient and expect Jesus to "balance everything out" later? Or is your response somewhere in between? Explain.**

(Needed: White index cards, soda straws, tape)

Have kids make "white flags" of surrender using index cards, straws, and tape. As you do, talk about the fact that the only logical response of the earthly army in this chapter would have been surrender—yet it kept fighting God. Ask: **What parts of your life are hardest to surrender to God? What do you think you'll gain by not surrendering? What do you think God will do if you do surrender?** Kids may or may not want to respond aloud. Encourage them to take these white flags with them as reminders that God is waiting for them to stop fighting Him and to discover what it means to really live "on His side."

ARMS RACE

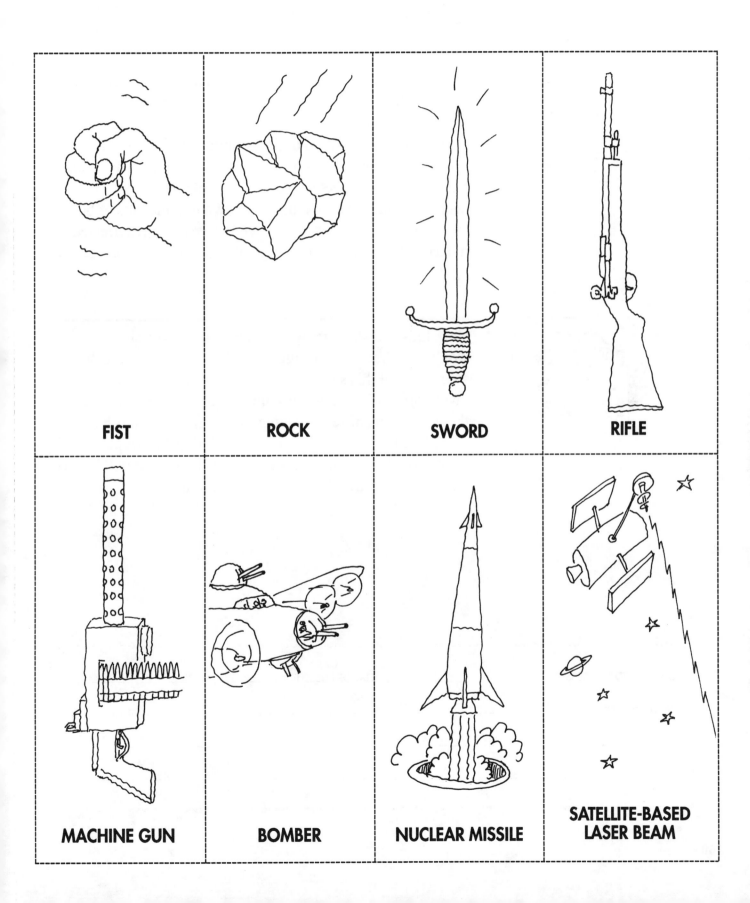

FIST

ROCK

SWORD

RIFLE

MACHINE GUN

BOMBER

NUCLEAR MISSILE

SATELLITE-BASED
LASER BEAM

REVELATION 20

Down with the Devil

After the beast and the false prophet have been eliminated (Chapter 19), the next figure to be dealt with is Satan himself. He is bound for a period of time, while the martyrs who resisted the beast are resurrected and reign with Jesus. When Satan is eventually released, he tries again to attack God's people. He fails and this time is thrown into the lake of burning sulfur. Soon afterward, the wicked dead are resurrected, judged, and sentenced at the "great white throne" judgment.

Have kids take "A Survey" (on the reproducible sheet). It won't take them long to figure out that there's something strange about this survey. All the choices are negative—involving death, sin, decay, pain, and disease. Explain that all these problems have something in common: Satan is behind them. The devil has caused untold suffering for people throughout history. In this session you'll see what will happen when it's "payback time" for our old enemy.

DATE I USED THIS SESSION _____ GROUP I USED IT WITH _____

NOTES FOR NEXT TIME _____

_____

_____

Q&A

1. Suppose gang members started making their presence known in your neighborhood. They want you to join, but you don't want to, so they make threatening comments about knowing where you live. You know they have knives, and you suspect they have guns. Each day it seems there are more of them. Which of the following would make you feel safer: (a) Police assurance to patrol more frequently; (b) joining the gang; (c) arming yourself to fight; or (d) discovering that the whole gang has been sent to prison for fifty years?

2. When Jesus returns (as described in chapter 19), **how will He deal with Satan's threatening presence** (vss. 1-3)? (Satan will be locked in the Abyss "for a thousand years.") **How do you think the world will change when the devil's not around?** [NOTE: Christians interpret the thousand-year reign of Jesus on earth (the "millennium") in various ways. Feel free to present your church's position on this issue. Your view may affect some of the following questions as well.]

3. What else will help convince people that the power of leadership has permanently changed hands (vss. 4-6)? (People who had been beheaded during the beast's rule will be resurrected and reign with Jesus. It will be an undeniable sign that *nothing* can permanently destroy the people of God.)

4. Do you ever have doubts that God will somehow make everything work out in your life? When do these feelings tend to appear? (Most people struggle with this at times. We tend to transfer to God our own inability to handle tough situations.)

5. After being bound during Christ's reign, Satan is released. He immediately recruits another massive army—numbering "like the sand on the seashore" (vss. 7, 8). Since God has to know this will happen, why do you think Satan will be released? (Maybe because final judgment is at hand, and people who grow up during the "thousand years" must choose whom to serve.)

6. But this time, as soon as God's people are threatened, what happens (vss. 9, 10)? (Fire destroys the armies, and Satan is thrown into the lake of burning sulfur.)

7. Do you see any indication here—or anywhere else in the Bible—to support the image we've all seen of Satan as the *ruler* of hell? (No. In fact, according to Jesus, the lake of fire was created for the devil and his angels [Matthew 25:41]. And here in verse 10 we are told that their torment will last forever.)

8. After the dead are resurrected comes the "great white throne" judgment. What will be the result of this event (vss. 11-15)? (Those whose names are not found in the book of life are thrown into the lake of fire.) **How can a loving God pass a sentence like this?** (God is also a just judge. If a human judge let all defendants off, regardless of their crimes or their lack of remorse, he or she would quickly be removed from the bench. It's not *pleasant* to declare someone guilty and pass sentence, but it is *fair*. Sometimes God doesn't get the same consideration from people that human judges do.)

Read verse 15 again. Ask: **What do you think the book of life is like? If it contains more than names, what might it have to say about you?** Explain that God is not a heartless record-keeper gathering evidence to convict us. He's a loving and forgiving Father. Though the book of life exists, it's much better to maintain a current relationship with Jesus than to be worried every minute about whether God is writing down something bad about us. When we know we've done something wrong, we need to confess it, make it right with God or with the other person, and get on with our lives. Ask: **How can you be sure that your name is in the book of life?** (Put your faith in Jesus Christ—while you still can [see John 3:14-18; Acts 16:31].) Have a time of silent prayer to allow students to confess sin or to place their faith in Christ for the first time.

A SURVEY

1. Which of the following would you like best?

    a. Strep throat
    b. Chicken pox
    c. Stomach flu
    d. Mumps

2. Which of the following foods do you enjoy most?

    a. Mold
    b. Scum
    c. Rust
    d. Anything rotten

3. Which of the following vacation spots would you prefer?

    a. Chernobyl
    b. A toxic waste dump
    c. The wreck of the Titanic
    d. Prison

4. Which of the following qualities do you appreciate most in others?

    a. Envy
    b. Lying
    c. Greed
    d. Hate

5. Which of the following do you find most amusing?

    a. Slavery
    b. War
    c. AIDS
    d. Drunk driving

6. Which of the following would you find most fun?

    a. Being robbed at gunpoint
    b. Being addicted to crack cocaine
    c. Having a migraine headache for two weeks
    d. Severe depression

7. Which of the following would you prefer?

    a. Dying of cancer
    b. Dying in a car accident
    c. Dying in a drive-by shooting
    d. Dying in a plane crash

REVELATION 21

Dream House

After the permanent removal of Satan, the "white throne" judgment, and the destruction of the earth, God provides a new heaven and new earth. John also witnesses a new city—a Holy City—"coming down out of heaven." His description of its size and splendor is unlike anything ever seen. This will be "the dwelling of God . . . with men," and entrance is available only to those who have put their trust in Him.

(Needed: Real estate ads, tape)

Before the session, cut as many home advertisements from the newspaper real estate section as you can. Post these around your meeting place. As kids arrive, give them pens and paper. Have them wander around, looking at the ads for ideas, as you say: **Write an ad for your "dream house." What kind of building would it be? Where would it be? What "extras" would come with the house?** When everyone is finished, collect the papers. Read one at a time, and see if group members can guess whose each one is. Then explain that, in spite of all the luxurious descriptions kids may have provided, the one in this chapter is sure to be even more impressive.

DATE I USED THIS SESSION _____ GROUP I USED IT WITH _____

NOTES FOR NEXT TIME _____

_____

_____

1. What's the most memorable building you've ever visited? Why does it stand out in your mind?

2. Most of us tend to wish we had more than we do. Sometimes we wonder if God knows what we're feeling, or if He cares about us. How can we be sure He does (vss. 1-4)? (When God created people, He had a special, close relationship with them. Sin separated us from Him for a long time, but He's creating a new place where we can interact with Him personally.)

3. God is making "everything new" (vs. 5). What are some situations you're facing that you wish could be made "new" right away? (Discuss some of these things. Remind kids that while perfection won't come until the time described in this chapter, God can make our bad situations *better* now. We may feel pain, but relying on God more completely can give us hope.)

4. How will it be possible for people to get along in heaven when they can't seem to do so here (vss. 6-8)? (Some of the "problem" people won't be in heaven (vs. 8). The rest of us, who have also sinned but have been forgiven through Christ, will no longer be bothered by the sinful natures we had on earth. It isn't clear exactly how this will happen. In any case, it's a good idea to start getting along now.)

5. If you knew your parents were building an incredible house for your family to live in, would you be willing to stay temporarily in a "dump"? Explain. (Compare this situation to living on earth until we eventually get to the city God has designed.)

6. A detailed description of the New Jerusalem is provided in verses 9-21. You may not recognize some of the precious stones listed, but what are some of the clear facts about this city? (The jewels described are different colors, and large portions of the city are "pure gold, as pure as glass." To envision such a place being illuminated by "the glory of God" [vs. 11] allows us to anticipate a place unlike anything we've ever seen.)

7. Why bother with all this fancy housing? Isn't God just interested in right, wrong, and obedience? (He's the most creative Being in the universe—and elsewhere. His work on the *old* earth also shows us that He values beauty and variety. This is another reason to praise Him—which we'll do a lot in our new home.)

8. If you translate the length of "12,000 stadia" into current measurement, you discover the city is about 1,400 *miles* long. It's also that wide and that high. What might that suggest about its shape? (Scholars debate whether it's a cube, which would reflect the shape of the Most Holy Place in the temple, or a pyramid, which some favor based on the description.)

9. How do you feel about being this close to God (vss. 22-27)? Why?

The reproducible sheet, "Your New Next-Door Neighbor," helps kids consider what it might be like to relate to the Lord more directly. When they finish, discuss their responses. Ask: **What can you do this week to relate to God in a more personal way? Would it help to get out in nature and talk to Him? Spend time praying without asking Him for anything? Write your idea on the back of your sheet. Then write a time when you'll actually try to do it this week. Fold your paper up and put it in your pocket as a reminder.**

Your New Next-Door Neighbor

If you've received Jesus, you'll someday discover that "now the dwelling of God is with men, and He will live with them" (Revelation 21:3). Then you'll *really* feel close to God—because He'll be right down the street. But what if it happened today? What if, when you got home from this meeting, you discovered that Jesus had moved into the place next door to yours?

Day 1   Jesus wants to meet all your friends and start hanging around with you—doing whatever you usually do and talking about whatever you usually talk about. Do you think this is a good idea? Explain.

Day 2   In the morning, after you've been out on a date, Jesus waves as you head for the bus. He asks how things went on your date. How do you feel? What do you say? Why?

Day 3   You're watching TV when the doorbell rings. It's Jesus. He wants to know if He can join you. As you explain what your favorite TV shows are and why, do you think He would like them as much as you do? Why?

Day 4   You're about to go to the mall to spend some money you got for your birthday. Jesus wants to come along and see what you pick out. Will His presence influence your purchases? Why or why not? If you have $40 to spend, how will you spend it?

REVELATION 22

Any Day Now

John's observations on God's Holy City continue with his description of the river of life and the tree of life. He records Jesus' reminder that He is coming soon and His command for us to respond to the "revelation" that has been passed on to us. Finally, John concludes with a warning not to add to or take away from what God had given him to write.

(Needed: Two boxes of chocolates; tray of healthful refreshments)

Have a chocolate-eating contest. Let two contestants dive into a couple of boxes of "bonbon"-type candies. Whoever eats the most in one minute is the winner. (The prize is any left-over chocolates.) Ask the contestants: **How do you feel? How many chocolates did you actually enjoy? About how many did you eat before you got tired of them?** Discuss with the whole group the idea some people have of heaven—that it's a place where you "pig out" on whatever you want, forever. Point out that this chapter gives us a very different view. Then serve some healthful but appealing refreshments to the group, noting that even things that are "good for us" can be enjoyable.

DATE I USED THIS SESSION _____ GROUP I USED IT WITH _____

NOTES FOR NEXT TIME _____

_____

_____

1. When do you like knowing in advance what's going to happen? (When somebody's trying to scare you; when you have to take a test; when you need something to look forward to, etc.) **When do you *not* like to know?** (When you're reading a book or watching a movie, etc.)

2. As Christians, we know what will happen to the world and its people . . . eventually. How should that affect the way we live? (We should have more confidence as we face hard times; we should be more eager to help others know the truth about Jesus and to grow spiritually.)

3. For people who put their faith in Jesus, what's in store (vss. 1-5)? (Eternal life in the presence of God, with the river of life, the tree of life, and no more sin.) **Does the symbolism here make it hard for you to get enthused about these benefits, or is enough of it clear to you? Explain.**

4. What do most people hope heaven is like? (Many hope it will be a place to do whatever they want, like an amusement park or eternal vacation.) **How does that compare with John's description?** (Serving and reigning with God, not being entertained, is the real focus.)

5. If you were in John's place and getting this "sneak preview," would you think it was too good to be true? What kept John from feeling this way (vs. 6)? (The angel kept assuring him.)

6. It's pretty hard to understand all the things in Revelation. Would it be better to forget about it and concentrate on other parts of the Bible (vss. 7-11)? Why or why not? (No. Jesus Himself reminds us that He is coming soon, and that we should know and obey what is taught in Revelation. The angel reminded John not to seal up what he had seen, "because the time is near.")

7. If we truly believe Jesus, that He is coming soon (vss. 12-16), do you think we as a group need to be doing anything different? How about you as an individual?

8. Does what you've read of Revelation lead you to think it's very hard to make it into heaven? Explain. (It's impossible for those who harden their hearts against God.) Do you think you meet the requirements, as expressed in the invitation in verse 17? Why or why not? (All are invited, and the offer is "free." That's why it's so tragic when people refuse to yield their wills to God.)

9. Should we focus on the "good" parts of Revelation (like heaven) and downplay the parts about plagues, the lake of burning sulfur, etc. (vss. 18-21)? Why or why not? (John makes it clear that we should not add to or take away from the prophecy he was shown.)

10. After everything John has seen, he closes his account with the short prayer, "Come, Lord Jesus" (vs. 20). Are you as eager as John was to pray this prayer? Why or why not?

Hand out the reproducible sheet, "R.S.V.P." Encourage kids to consider it carefully, to read the two asterisked passages, to check the appropriate box, and to fill in the blanks. Then have them turn the "reply card" in to you. Discuss the fact that God gives us two choices—accept His Son or reject His Son. Say: **Some people think it's not fair for God to keep anyone out of heaven. Do you think it would be fair for God to force people to spend eternity with Him, when they've shown on earth that they don't want to be with Him or to worship Him?** Follow up later with any kids who checked boxes other than the first one.

R.S.V.P.

Take Advantage of This Once-in-a-Lifetime FREE Offer!

☐ **YES** I'd like to live forever with God in the incredibly beautiful place He's prepared for me. I understand that I will get to worship Him, serve Him, and rule with Him. I will be allowed to do this because I have put my trust in Jesus Christ, God's Son, who died for my sins.

☐ **YES** I'd like to get all those great benefits. But I need more information about how to put my trust in Jesus.

☐ **NO** I don't want to live forever with God. It sounds boring.*

☐ **NO** I don't want to worship God forever. It's bad enough having to do it here.*

☐ **NO** I don't want to serve God or rule with Him forever. It sounds like too much work.*

☐ **HEY** wait a minute! Don't I get another choice? Can't I go to heaven and just sort of goof around and forget all that serving stuff? Can't I make up my own idea of heaven and get there however I want to?*

*See John 3:17, 18; Revelation 20:15.

NAME_____

ADDRESS_____

PHONE_____

Act now! This special offer could end anytime—when your life on earth does.